WALKING DEVON

THE
RIVER AXE

Richard Easterbrook
&
Geoff Broadhurst

EASTERHURST PUBLICATIONS LTD

Photographs by Richard Easterbrook
Sketches by Geoff Broadhurst

ISBN 0 9538272 0 8
© Richard Easterbrook & Geoff Broadhurst 2000

First published in 2000 by Easterhurst Publications Ltd
11, Warwick Close, Feniton, Devon, EX14 3DT.

Note:- The information given in this book has been provided in good faith and is intended for general guidance only. Whilst all reasonable efforts have been made to ensure that details were correct at the time of publication, the authors and publisher cannot accept responsibility for any inaccuracies which are a result of changes occurring after going to print. It remains the responsibility of individuals undertaking any outdoor pursuits, to approach them with caution, and if inexperienced, to do so under proper supervision. The walk in this book, is, in the main not particularly strenuous, but you should ensure that you are fit enough to complete any section you embark upon.

Cover Photographs
Front - Axmouth Harbour from Axe Bridge
Back - Cloakham Bridge near Axminster

PREFACE

After air and sunlight, water is mankind's most precious commodity. Its presence, be it in the form of ocean, lake, river or garden pond seems to exert an unfailing magnetism and fascination to all those who venture near it. Devon is fortunate in having more than its fair share of water, with its two coastlines attracting a host of visitors every year. Inland numerous rivers rise, principally from the heights of Dartmoor, Exmoor or the Blackdown Hills, before winding their way to the sea. With few exceptions the rivers complete their journeys at one of Devon's eleven estuaries, more than in any other County in England.

Walking is undoubtedly one of the most popular outdoor leisure pursuits in this country, and, by using the network of Public Rights of Way, a means of access to the countryside is available which enables it to be enjoyed by all. There is therefore, no better way than to walk along Devon's rivers and at the same time explore and enjoy the delightful and varied countryside through which they flow. The idea for this book, and others planned for the series, originated as a result of us deciding to do just that. There are many excellent books, guides and information packs on the subject of Devon's rivers, or parts of Devon's rivers. However we could find none that gave a 'walking boots eye' view of what is to be encountered when walking an entire river from source to sea. In this book every stile, gate and footbridge along the way is mentioned, in fact all that you pass by, go through, over, under or across, by walking the described route.

Through this series of books we wish to share with you the immense enjoyment, pleasure and sense of achievement that walking these rivers gave us, and hope that the books will encourage you to embark upon **WALKING DEVON'S RIVERS** yourself.

Richard Easterbrook
&
Geoff Broadhurst

AT THE TIME OF GOING TO PRINT THE FOLLOWING BOOKS
BY THE SAME AUTHORS
WERE IN THE COURSE OF PREPARATION

Walking Devon's Rivers

THE RIVER TEIGN
THE RIVER OTTER

Pub Walks & Crawls by Public Transport

EAST DEVON

ACKNOWLEDGEMENTS

This book was made possible with the help of many people. The Authors would like to extend their thanks to staff at Dorset, Somerset and Devon County Councils for their assistance when checking and verifying the rights of way information and also to staff at East Devon District Council for their input. Thanks are also due to the staff at the County Library in Exeter for their patience and enthusiasm in obtaining useful sources of information.

A special thank you must go to our good friends Sharon Macey and Paul Livsey for carrying out the unenviable task of walking the route using only the directions and sketches given in this book. We are glad to say they arrived at Axmouth Harbour none the worst for their experiences ! Thanks are also due to Wendy Lane for proof reading the text. To those who have also helped but we have not mentioned - thank you.

CONTENTS

PART 1
GENERAL ADVICE FOR WALKERS

EQUIPMENT, SAFETY and COMFORT

The walk generally involves either road or field walking and ranges from a few fairly steep sections to the more gentle rambles by the Axe itself. Although not quite the same as the rigours of moorland walking it is still necessary to wear appropriate footwear and clothing. You should also carry a waterproof and spare dry clothing in case the weather changes and possibly a small first aid kit. As there are only a few places to obtain food and drink along the way you should carry sufficient supplies with you dependent on the distance you intend to travel. We also recommend you take Ordnance Survey Explorer Map 116 (Bridport & Lyme Regis) with you as this covers the whole walk and will assist in identifying features along the route.

PUBLIC RIGHTS OF WAY

The Definitive Map

All Public Rights of Way are shown on a 'Definitive Map'. This is the legal record of these Rights of Way for each County. It was produced in England and Wales as a result of the 1949 National Parks and Access to the Countryside Act. Local Authorities are obliged to keep these up to date to show any legal changes to the network. Each Right of Way has a unique number according to the Parish it is in and the type of Right of Way – i.e. Axminster, Footpath 20 or Beaminster, Bridleway 3. Ordnance Survey Explorer, Landranger and Outdoor Leisure Maps show most public rights of way but will obviously not show any changes made after the maps were published.

The Rights of Way used by the route described in this book were checked against the relevant Definitive Maps as follows:- Somerset - June 1999; Dorset - July 1999; Devon - November 1999.

Types of Rights of Way

Three categories of Public Right of Way exist, which, along with their basic legal definitions, are as follows:-

Footpath (coloured Yellow)
A highway over which the public have a right of way on foot only.

Bridleway (coloured Blue)
A highway over which the public have the right of way on foot, or to ride or lead a horse (or mule or donkey). Pedal cycles are also allowed but cyclists have to give way to pedestrians and riders. There is no right to drive a vehicle.

Byway (coloured Red)
   A highway over which the public not only have a right of way as for bridleways but for vehicular use as well.

A further right of way known as a **'Permissive Path'** (coloured Green) also exists, but the right of passage is at the discretion of the landowner and can be withdrawn at anytime.

The Use of Public Rights of Way

A Right of Way is what it implies – a right of passage over the ground. You do not have the right to roam at will or use the ground for any other purpose. Although Right of Ways should be kept open and unobstructed you should bear in mind that landowners are not obliged to provide a good surface or signpost the route across their land. You are required to keep to the correct line at all times, but this is not always possible, or is sometimes impractical to do so. For example, you may come across a deliberate illegal obstruction such as a barbed wire fence, or simply a fallen tree or branch. In either case, you are allowed to remove the obstacle sufficiently to get past or you may take a short alternative route around it. You are also permitted to take a short detour, (keeping close to a field boundary wherever possible) to overcome a broken stile or footbridge for example.

THE COUNTRY CODE

Remember that by using the paths properly and following the Country Code, you are much less likely to come across any problems.

- Enjoy the countryside and respect its life and work.
- Guard against all risk of fire
- Fasten all gates
- Keep your dogs under close control, and always on a lead when there is livestock around
- Keep to the public paths
- Use gates and stiles to cross fences, hedges and walls
- Leave livestock, crops and machinery alone
- Take your litter home
- Help to keep all water clean
- Take special care on country roads - face oncoming traffic
- Protect wildlife, plants and trees

AND MOST IMPORTANT OF ALL

- **TAKE NOTHING**   -   but photographs and memories
- **LEAVE NOTHING**   -   but footprints

PART 2
THE ROUTE

THE COURSE OF THE RIVER AXE

Total length	24 miles
Source	Nr Broadleaze Farm at Grid Reference ST 497047
Finish	Axmouth Bridge at Grid Reference SY 254899
Height at Source	190 metres (623 feet)
Main Tributaries	Rivers Yarty and Coly

In reality the river has two principal sources, but it is generally accepted that it gurgles into existence in a copse near **Broadleaze Farm.** The Axe starts its journey in a slightly north-westerly direction and, after just a mile and a half, was of sufficient force to drive a mill at **Buckham.** The first 'stone' bridge spanning the Axe is reached a further mile and a half downstream at **Mosterton.** From here the river continues north-westerly, passing south of the tranquil hamlet of **Seaborough.** After another mile or so the Axe reaches the mill at **Clapton.** Passing below the small hamlet of **Wayford** the river starts to take a south-westerly course, with the valley becoming more clearly defined. The river now forms the boundaries of Dorset and Somerset as the distant hills of Devon come into view. The pleasant village of **Winsham** is soon reached followed by the small hamlet of **Ammerham** and then **Forde Abbey.** Built over 800 years ago the Abbey is the most complete Cistercian Monastic building in Britain still surviving as a residence. About a mile after leaving the Abbey the Axe passes through **Chard Junction**, where it takes a more meandering and southerly course as it strives to reach Devon. The hills forming the valley sides are now noticeably further apart as the river makes its way under Weycroft Bridge and the route of the Roman "Fosse Way". The Axe is spanned by the delightful single stone arch of Cloakham Bridge, before passing to the north-east of the market town of **Axminster**, world famous for its carpets. As it meanders on, first under 'Bow Bridge' and then the modern A35 road bridge, the Axe is joined by the first of its two larger tributaries, the River Yarty. By now the hills are wider apart forming an enlarged plain. The village of **Kilmington** nestles high on the western slopes with the Iron Age fort above **Musbury** commanding the skyline on the eastern side. Skirting the village of **Whitford** to the south-east, the Axe now flows directly south as it winds towards the final stages of its journey. After flowing under the A3052, the second of its larger tributaries, the River Coly, joins the Axe just below **Colyford**. By now the river has entered its tidal reaches, its wide estuary forming a haven for wildlife. The estuary is the most easterly in Devon, and is also the smallest, extending only two and a half miles southwards from its tidal limit just north of the A3052 road bridge to its mouth. The Seaton Tramway follows the western bank, whilst the small village of **Axmouth** sits on the opposite bank. Just two more bridges, alongside each other, span the Axe before it forms **Axmouth Harbour.** Haven Cliffs form a magnificent finale to the river's twenty four mile journey, as it squeezes through its narrow entrance and into the sea, to the east of **Seaton.**

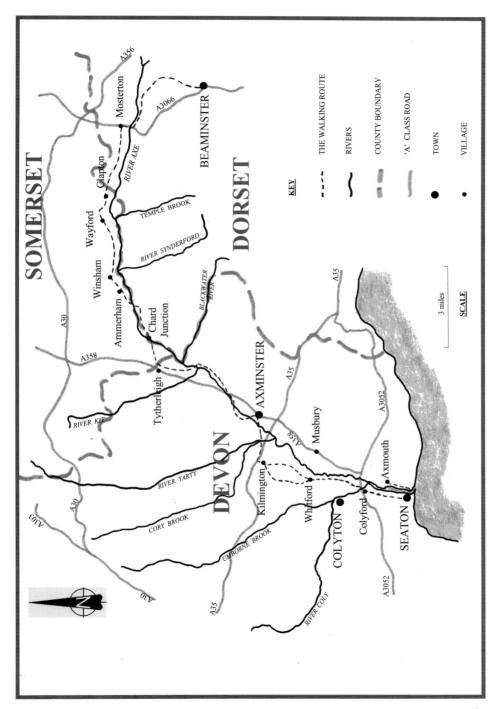

KEY

THE WALKING ROUTE

RIVERS

COUNTY BOUNDARY

'A' CLASS ROAD

TOWN

VILLAGE

SCALE

3 miles

SOMERSET

DORSET

DEVON

Mosterton

Clapton

Wayford

Winsham

Ammerham

Chard Junction

Tytherleigh

BEAMINSTER

AXMINSTER

Musbury

Axmouth

Kilmington

Whitford

Colyford

COLYTON

SEATON

RIVER AXE

TEMPLE BROOK

RIVER SYNDERFORD

BLACKWATER RIVER

RIVER KIT

RIVER YARTY

CORY BROOK

UMBORNE BROOK

RIVER COLY

A356

A3066

A30

A358

A35

A35

A3052

A3052

A35

A30

A303

A358

N

9

PART 3
THE WALK

WALK DETAILS

Total length	28.02 miles (max) 27.76 miles (min)
Start	Beaminster at Grid Reference ST 480013
Finish	Axmouth Harbour at Grid Reference SY 256897
Highest point reached	Buckham Down at 224 metres (735 feet)
Towns and Villages	Beaminster, Mosterton, Clapton, Winsham, Chard
on the route	Junction, Axminster, Kilmington, Colyford and Seaton.

The Axe is one of the many delightful and interesting rivers that form an integral part of Devon's unrivalled landscape. The river does however rise in Dorset, and forms that County's boundary with Somerset for the first part of its twenty four mile journey to the English Channel. However, along with its two main tributaries the Yarty and Coly, the Axe is contained principally within the south-eastern corner of Devon, flowing through the lush green fertile countryside that characterises that part of the County. Somewhat rather disappointingly, the derivation of the name 'Axe' simply signifies 'Water', and is probably of Phoenician origin.

WALK DESCRIPTIONS

The walk as described in this book is about twenty eight miles long. It has been designed as a continuous walk over 2 or 3 days but could be done in smaller sections or over a longer period. The descriptions and accompanying sketches which have been produced are based on a route which has been walked by us many times. We hope that the book will be of use to everyone who enjoys walking and that the descriptions and sketch maps present an easy to follow picture.

However, the passage of time can introduce changes at the hands of both man and nature; that signpost or stile may no longer be there, or that footbridge washed away. There is also the distinct possibility that a footpath may have become re-routed or even new ones introduced. For example, where a new bypass has been constructed or if changes in farming methods have to be accommodated. Most landowners tend to be very co-operative in keeping rights of way clear of obstruction. Indeed, not once during our walking did we come across any blatant obstruction.

The English seasons do of course present their own natural challenges to the walker, from the sometimes overgrown grass, nettles and brambles of summer, to the boggy and slippery surfaces in winter. Such seasonal problems are easily overcome by those wearing suitable gear. It should be specifically borne in mind that the Axe, and in particular its lower reaches, is very susceptible to flooding. This will inevitably result in very wet ground even after floodwater has receded. This will not only serve to

10

make some sections of the walk difficult, but in the extreme, impassable! Although we have not attempted to suggest possible diversions in this book, any experienced walker armed with the relevant Ordnance Survey map should have no difficulty in finding an alternative route should the need arise.

As far as possible, the walk has been deliberately routed to use only footpaths, bridleways and byways, but some road walking is inevitable. Where a 'permissive path' has been used it is indicated as such in the walk descriptions. The maps and descriptions, when read in conjunction with an Ordnance Survey Map, should make it possible for you to complete the walk without any problems. With a few exceptions, the route of the walk is reasonably well signposted and waymarked on the ground, but may not always be straightforward to follow without the aid of this book and map.

PLANNING YOUR WALK

For those of you who wish to complete the walk with the minimal amount of stops, we would suggest that you make it a two day walk; from Beaminster to Chard Junction on the first day, and then the remainder to Seaton or Axmouth on the second day. If however, you wish to spend time looking around the various places of interest along the way, we would suggest that you split the walk into three days, covering Beaminster to Winsham, Winsham to Axminster, and finally Axminster to Seaton (or Axmouth). It should be possible for you to cover each of these lengths in a day, to include refreshment stops etc, and still have ample time to look around. In either of the above cases, and with the lone walker in mind, we have taken into consideration the availability of car parking and public transport along the way. This ensures that no retracing of steps should be necessary to get back again. Our own preference was to leave a car at the 'finish' and then use public transport to get to the 'start'. There are two advantages in doing this; firstly, it acts as a good safeguard should the 'unexpected' happen, such as no bus turning up at the far end; secondly, it gives you the opportunity to ramble without having to keep an 'eye on the clock'.

USING THE SKETCHES
AND WALK DESCRIPTIONS

General

The whole walk from Beaminster to Seaton (or Axmouth) has been divided into eighteen sections. These have been largely determined by the need to clearly define the route using what we hope are concise, easy to follow notes and sketch maps. As a result each section covers approximately a mile and a half, the actual length being indicated at the head of the page immediately opposite the corresponding sketch map.

A ⬤ symbol indicates the start of paragraphs containing the actual walking directions, which are **highlighted in bold text.**

Places of Interest and Facilities

Brief descriptive notes on places and points of interest along the way are also included. Facilities available on or near the route have been indicated, either in the notes themselves, or on the sketch maps. To assist you in planning ahead we have, wherever possible, indicated the distance to the next available facilities.

Transport

Bus Stops and Service Numbers have been marked on the maps and afford the opportunity to break your journey if necessary. Because bus services and times are liable to change frequently, only the current services and their operators have been listed in **Part 4,** along with Taxi operators.

THE START OF YOUR WALK

Although over a mile and a half from the source of the river we have started the walk at Beaminster for convenience. The town is relatively easy to get to by public transport or by car. Should you use the latter means there is parking available near to the main square. As we have suggested earlier however, it may be advisable to leave your car at your planned 'finish' point. Beaminster is a delightful example of a small Dorset town. Starting here provides an opportunity to look around the town itself before stocking up for the walk ahead.

KEY TO SYMBOLS USED ON SKETCH MAPS

FP	**Footpath**		**FB**	**Footbridge**
BW	**Bridleway**		**Wk**	**Waymark**
WC	**Public Convenience**		**PO**	**Post Office**
G	**Garage** (selling refreshments etc)		**LC**	**Level Crossing**
S	**Shop** (in villages only)		**PH**	**Public House**
TIC	**Tourist Information Centre**		**•**	**Signpost**
•—•	**Gate or Stile**		——	**Wall** (brick, stone or concrete)
] [	**Bridge**		⊔⊔⊔	**Fence** (wood, iron or wire)
■■■■	**Railway**		aaaa	**Hedge or Scrub**
(	**Public Telephone**		⋺⋵	**Panoramic View**

— — — — **The Walking Route**

Beaminster

A.D.Mills in his book 'Dorset Place Names' suggests that the name 'Beaminster' is derived from "a church associated with a woman named Bebbe", although others suggest 'Beam Ministre' as a church in a wood. Beaminster is a small but prosperous market town tucked away in the West Dorset hills at the head of the Brit Valley. Once dependant on a thriving cloth industry the town was devastated by fires in 1644, 1684 and again in 1781, the one in 1644 being started deliberately by Prince Rupert. As a result little remains of some of the original and finest 17th century houses, but there are many fine examples of Georgian buildings and 17th century cottages to be seen amongst the town's 200 or so listed buildings. The present church of St Mary dates from the 15th century and stands on the site of its Norman predecessor. History records that in 1685, after the Battle of Sedgemoor, King James II used the tower as a gallows in order to show the townsfolk what would become of disloyal subjects. One of Beaminster's

St Mary's Church, Beaminster

most famous sons was the much travelled Thomas Hinde. Born in 1775, Hinde travelled to France when he was seventeen and found work in a brandy business in Jarnac. He had the foresight to marry the boss's daughter, and having knuckled his way in, he eventually became the owner. He gave his name to 'Cognac Hinde' long considered as a connoisseur's brandy. Hinde died in 1822. Three quarters of a mile south of the town, just off the A3066, is Parnham House. Although having a long history it is now the home of the famous Makepeace cabinet making business where items are individually designed and built. A school for young craftsmen was set up here in 1977 and visitors are welcome to watch the community at work and enjoy the surrounding fourteen acres of gardens. Other nearby places of interest, not on the route, include:- **Horn Park Gardens, Mapperton Gardens** and **Broadwindsor Craft & Design Centre,** details of which can be obtained from Beaminster Library or local Tourist Information Centres.

*Note:- Before setting off from Beaminster, you should bear in mind that there are no further facilities for walkers until you reach Mosterton **(approximately 4 miles)***

1. BEAMINSTER to BUCKHAM DOWN

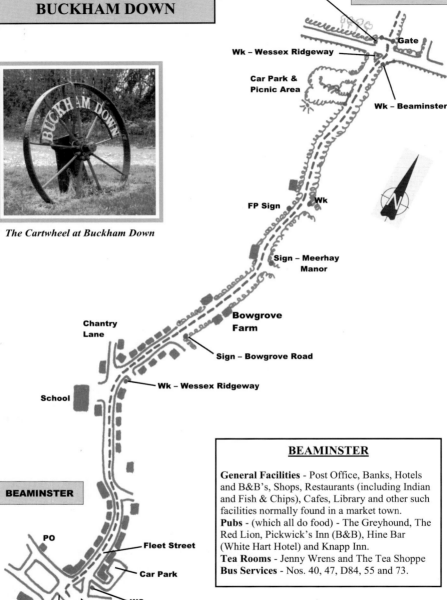

FP Sign – Chedington & Mosterton

BUCKHAM DOWN

Gate

Wk – Wessex Ridgeway

Car Park & Picnic Area

Wk – Beaminster

FP Sign Wk

Sign – Meerhay Manor

Bowgrove Farm

Chantry Lane

Sign – Bowgrove Road

Wk – Wessex Ridgeway

School

BEAMINSTER

PO

Fleet Street

Car Park

WC

Church

Bus Stop

The Square

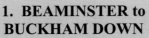

The Cartwheel at Buckham Down

BEAMINSTER

General Facilities - Post Office, Banks, Hotels and B&B's, Shops, Restaurants (including Indian and Fish & Chips), Cafes, Library and other such facilities normally found in a market town.
Pubs - (which all do food) - The Greyhound, The Red Lion, Pickwick's Inn (B&B), Hine Bar (White Hart Hotel) and Knapp Inn.
Tea Rooms - Jenny Wrens and The Tea Shoppe
Bus Services - Nos. 40, 47, D84, 55 and 73.

From 'The Square' take 'Fleet Street' to the north. This part of the route follows the 'Wessex Ridgeway'. Look out for the old Methodist Chapel which has been converted into two cottages and Star Cottage which was originally the Star Public House. **Follow the road left by the stream and go past the playing fields on your left as far as the school. Just past the school, follow the road right** (waymarked) **and start climbing the hill** (through the areas known as 'Newtown' and then 'Hurst') **and then go straight on up the signed 'Bowgrove Road'. Continue climbing up the lane heading north past 'Bowgrove Farm' and carry on until just past a footpath sign on your left. When you come to a junction with a waymark** ('Wessex Ridgeway and Brit Valley Circular Walk') **bear left, continuing up the lane which soon becomes an earth and rubble track enclosed by trees. After about a hundred yards or so, a stream runs down the left-hand side. After more climbing, you will approach obvious signs of being near the top. However just before reaching the top, there is a wooden gate on your left shortly followed by a car park entrance on the same side**. Either of these will lead you into a picnic area (formerly a rubbish tip) offering absolutely superb views over Dorset all the way to the sea. You are now at Buckham Down. **Leaving the picnic site continue on up the lane for the last few yards until you reach the main road and a triangular area.** Notice the old cartwheel with the inscription "Buckham Down". Also located on the triangular area is a waymark sign indicating that 'The Wessex Ridgeway' turns right here.

Beaminster and beyond viewed from Buckham Down

15

2. BUCKHAM DOWN to BAKER'S MILL FARM

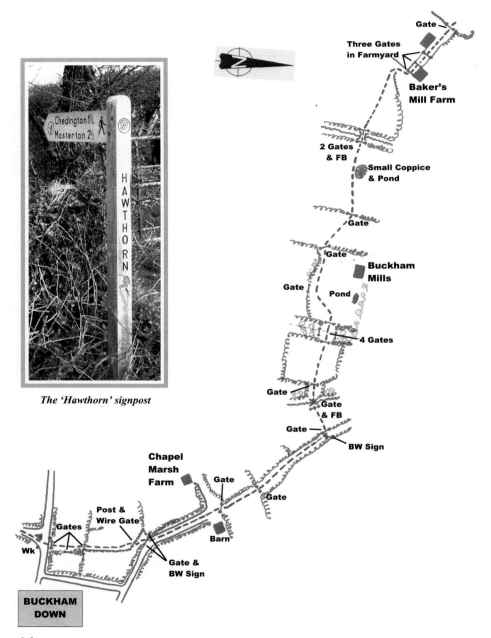

The 'Hawthorn' signpost

Chedington 1¼
Mosterton 2½

HAWTHORN

Gate

Three Gates
in Farmyard

Baker's
Mill Farm

2 Gates
& FB

Small Coppice
& Pond

Gate

Gate

Buckham
Mills

Gate

Pond

4 Gates

Gate

Gate
& FB

Gate

BW Sign

Chapel
Marsh
Farm

Gate

Gate

Post &
Wire Gate

Gates

Barn

Wk

Gate &
BW Sign

BUCKHAM
DOWN

⚫ **From the triangular area cross the road to the footpath signpost 'Hawthorn'** (Chedington - 1¼ miles, Mosterton - 2½ miles). **Go through the metal gate to the right of the signpost and into the field. Continue straight ahead and downhill, keeping the hedge on your right, to a metal gate** (waymarked). **Go through the metal gate and down a track which has a post and wire fence on the right.** Over to the right you can see a wooded combe which is between 'West' and 'East Axnoller' Farms. This is where the River Axe has its source. **Towards the end of the track go through a collapsible post and wire gate towards two metal gates. Take the right-hand gate onto a surfaced track by a signpost.** Here your route has joined the 'Monarch's Way'.

The 'Monarch's Way' is 609 miles long and is based on the route taken by Charles II during his escape after the Battle of Worcester in 1651. It starts at Worcester itself, and takes in Stratford-upon-Avon, the Cotswolds, Mendips and then along the south coast from Charmouth in Dorset to Shoreham-by-Sea in West Sussex. Further details can be obtained from the Monarch's Way Association, 15, Alison Road, Lapal, Halesowen, B62 0AT.

⚫ **Bear left when through the gate and follow the track until it turns left near a barn on the right. At this point go straight ahead through a metal gate** (waymarked) **into a field and down the left-hand side following the hedge. At the bottom of the field go through a waymarked wooden gate into a green lane between high hedges. After about four hundred yards or so you will come to a bridleway signpost on your right. Turn left here through a small gate and into a field. Go straight across the field to a waymarked gate leading to a broken sleeper footbridge. Go over this and another footbridge into a short track through a copse and on to a waymarked gate which leads into a field. Go across the field, keeping the hedge on your right, to a metal gate in the far right-hand corner. Go through the gate into a small coppice where another footpath crosses at right angles. Go straight ahead to another metal gate into a field. Follow the left-hand hedge across the field through piles of rubbish and old farm machinery, ignoring the gate in the left-hand hedge.** To your right is 'Buckham Mills', its pond, and a first glimpse of the River Axe. **Continue to keep the hedge on your left to a metal gate in the left-hand corner of the field. Go through the gate and straight across the field to a metal gate on the far side. Go through and head straight across a large field, passing to the left of a coppice with a pond in the middle, and on to a small gate on the far side. Go through this and over a footbridge to another gate** (waymarked) **into a field. Go diagonally right across the field heading for the buildings of 'Baker's Mill Farm'. On approaching the farm** the Monarch's Way turns left but **you continue into the farmyard through a metal gate.** (There is a yellow waymark on the wooden fence before the gate). **Go straight ahead through two more metal gates in the yard and then continue to another metal gate at the far end.**

17

3. BAKER'S MILL FARM to SEABOROUGH DAIRY

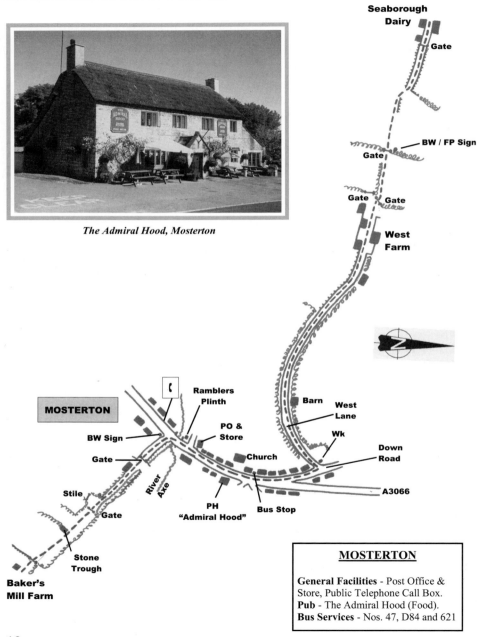

The Admiral Hood, Mosterton

Seaborough Dairy

Gate

BW / FP Sign

Gate

Gate   Gate

West Farm

MOSTERTON

Ramblers Plinth

Barn   West Lane

BW Sign

PO & Store

Wk

Gate

Church

Down Road

Stile

River Axe

A3066

Gate

PH "Admiral Hood"   Bus Stop

Stone Trough

Baker's Mill Farm

MOSTERTON

General Facilities - Post Office & Store, Public Telephone Call Box.
Pub - The Admiral Hood (Food).
Bus Services - Nos. 47, D84 and 621

⬤ **After passing through the gate** (waymarked) **and into a field keep to the right-hand hedge and go through a gap by a stone trough into the next field. Still keeping to the right-hand hedge** (alongside a small stream) **head for a metal gate in the corner of the field where the field narrows. Go through the gate** (waymarked) **into a green lane with a stream** (which joins the Axe in Mosterton) **running down the right-hand side. Follow the lane,** which can be very wet at times, **down to farm buildings** on the left **where it becomes a surfaced road. Go through a metal gate and follow the lane down to the main road** (A3066) **at Mosterton. At the main road turn right** over the Axe **and go up the hill and through the village.**

Mosterton

A.D. Mills gives Mosterton's derivation as "Thorn tree belonging to a man named Mort". Situated in lovely countryside Mosterton can easily be confused with its Somerset counterpart of Misterton which is only two miles to the north. The 'Admiral Hood' public house stands on the site of what was formerly the 'New Inn' which was destroyed by fire in 1955. The 'New Inn' in turn had been built on the site of a Georgian house which was occupied by the Hood family, whose name is recorded as being at Mosterton since the sixteenth century. The pub itself is named after Admiral Viscount Samuel Hood (1724 - 1816), one of a distinguished naval family after whom several British warships have subsequently been named. The most famous of these was the one sunk by the 'Bismarck' in 1941. The present pub was rebuilt in the original style and is a listed building. Across the road from the 'Admiral Hood' is the Church of St Mary. The church was rebuilt on its present site in 1833, but internally it still retains its original fittings. The stained glass window featuring a tractor and combine harvester is comparatively recent having been installed in 1975.

Note:- Before setting off from Mosterton, you should bear in mind that, apart from a Telephone Call Box at Seaborough, there are no further facilities for walkers until you reach Clapton (approximately 3½ miles)

⬤ **Go past the 'Admiral Hood'** on the right, **and the Church** on the left, **and carry on up the hill. Go past the 'Eeles Pottery'** on the right, **and at the end of the village turn left into 'Down Road' and then almost immediately left into 'West Lane'** (signed as a bridleway) **which leads to 'West Farm'. Follow the lane all the way to the farm. Go through the farmyard in front of the farmhouse until you come to two metal gates. Take the higher** (right-hand) **of these two gates and follow the left-hand side of the field keeping the hedge close to your left. Carry on to the end of the field to a small wooden gate and a signpost** (Seaborough - straight ahead, Littlewindsor - left). **Go through the gate and straight across the field. As it starts to go downhill join the surfaced farm track between post and wire fences down to a metal gate and into the farmyard.** You are now at 'Seaborough Dairy'. **Go through the farmyard and continue on to the surfaced road at the far end of the yard.**

19

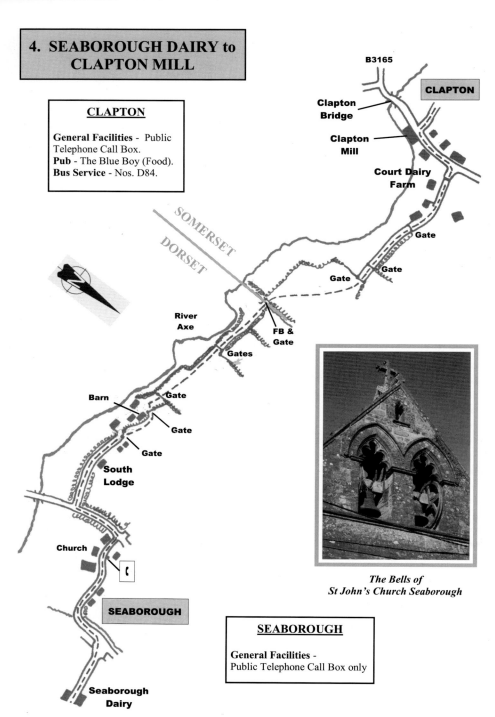

4. SEABOROUGH DAIRY to CLAPTON MILL

B3165

CLAPTON

Clapton Bridge

Clapton Mill

Court Dairy Farm

CLAPTON

General Facilities - Public Telephone Call Box.
Pub - The Blue Boy (Food).
Bus Service - Nos. D84.

SOMERSET
DORSET

Gate

Gate

Gate

River Axe

FB & Gate

Gates

Barn

Gate

Gate

Gate

South Lodge

Church

SEABOROUGH

Seaborough Dairy

The Bells of
St John's Church Seaborough

SEABOROUGH

General Facilities -
Public Telephone Call Box only

Follow the farm road down to a road junction by the farm name on a metal gate and a signpost (Mosterton - 1½ miles). **Turn left onto the road** (not the parallel track) **and continue on towards Seaborough.** The Axe can be seen down to your left. **Carry on through Seaborough passing the Church and Manor House,** both on your left, **to a T junction.**

Seaborough

A.D.Mills gives Seaborough's derivation as meaning seven hills or barrows. Seaborough is a small hamlet made up of several large surrounding farms. The Manor House and the tiny Church of St John are situated in the centre of the hamlet.

Turn left at the junction and go downhill towards the river. As you near the river turn right onto a surfaced road (unsigned apart from blue bridleway arrows on a telegraph pole). **Go along this road past 'South Lodge' and then the entrance to 'West Lea'** both on your right. **Carry straight on towards a farmyard. As you near the farmyard, go through a waymarked metal gate on your right and into a field.**

The Axe at Seaborough

Keep close to the fence on your left **and when past the barn turn immediately left to another waymarked metal gate. Go through the gate onto a track. Turn right and go along the track to a metal gate** (waymarked) **and go through into a field. Keep to the left-hand edge,** which runs parallel to the River Axe for a short distance, **until the path bears slightly right. When you come to two metal gates go through the left-hand gate onto a short track,** where you are joined by the Axe again, **which eventually opens out into a field. Keep close to the right-hand edge until you go over a piped ditch to a small metal gate. Go through the gate,** which marks the Dorset and Somerset Boundary, **and head diagonally right uphill across the field to a metal gate in the far corner. Go through this gate and two others on the track down to 'Court Dairy Farm'. Go past the farm, over a cattle grid, and down to the main road** (B3165). If you wish to visit the 'Blue Boy' or 'Clapton Court' you should turn right here; both are a few hundred yards up the road on your right. **To continue the walk turn left and go along the road towards the river and 'Clapton Mill'.**

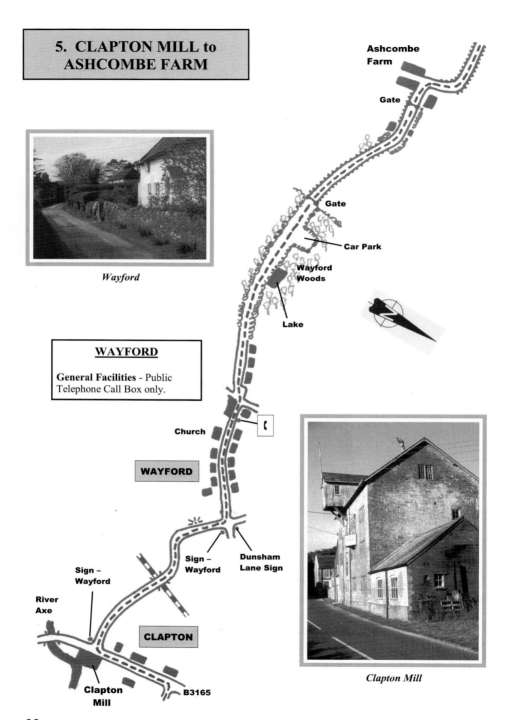

5. CLAPTON MILL to ASHCOMBE FARM

Wayford

WAYFORD

General Facilities - Public Telephone Call Box only.

Ashcombe Farm

Gate

Gate

Car Park

Wayford Woods

Lake

Church

WAYFORD

Sign – Wayford

Sign – Wayford

Dunsham Lane Sign

River Axe

CLAPTON

Clapton Mill

B3165

Clapton Mill

Clapton

Clapton is a small settlement composed of Estate buildings and the Mill, centred around 'Clapton Court'. The 10 acres of gardens are one of the most interesting and beautiful in Somerset. Although they are privately owned the gardens are open to the public and are well worth visiting. *Usually open three afternoons a week between April and September - Telephone 01460 73220 for details*

*Note:- Before setting off from Clapton, you should bear in mind that, apart from a Telephone Call Box at Wayford, there are no further facilities for walkers until you reach Winsham (**approximately 2¾ miles**)*

At the Mill turn right into the road 'Chard Lane' **on the opposite side.** (signed to Wayford). **Go up the hill, passing over the railway, and continue on until you get to a crossroads.** Here there is a superb view along the Axe Valley. **At the crossroads turn left,** signposted Wayford, **go downhill and then carry on through Wayford itself.** You have now joined the 'Liberty Trail' which you will follow all the way to just beyond 'Forde Abbey'.

The 'Liberty Trail' is 28 miles long and runs from Ham Hill in South Somerset to the Dorset Coast at Lyme Regis. It is based upon the route taken by the protestant supporters of The Duke of Monmouth in their bid to make him King. An excellent information pack describing the route using maps and text directions is available from Tourist Information Centres and South Somerset District Council.

Wayford

Wayford lies nestled on a hillside overlooking the Axe valley and is a tiny hamlet at the end of a no through road, although pedestrians can continue on to Winsham. The Daubeney family acquired the manor in the early 16th century. Next to the Manor House is St Michael's Church which probably had a 13th century foundation, its most noticeable feature, apart from the 'pebbledash' rendering, being the tiny wooden shingle-clad bellcote which houses two bells.

Passing the Manor House on your left continue straight on along the road until you reach Wayford Woods on your right. The woods are administered by a charitable trust and are open to the public. **Continuing on, you will come to a waterfall on your right** which comes from the ornamental lake which can be viewed by going up the steps nearby. Also nearby, near the end of the woods, is a car park. **As you reach the end of the woods the road** is signposted as a 'Private Road' to 'Ashcombe Farm' and 'Hey Farm', and **becomes bounded by a post and wire fence on either side. Continue on this road all the way to 'Ashcombe Farm'. As you approach the farm stay on the surfaced road** (the permissive path) instead of going across the fields on your right as indicated on the Explorer Map. **Go through and around the farmyard and continue on the road which bears left up a slight hill.**

23

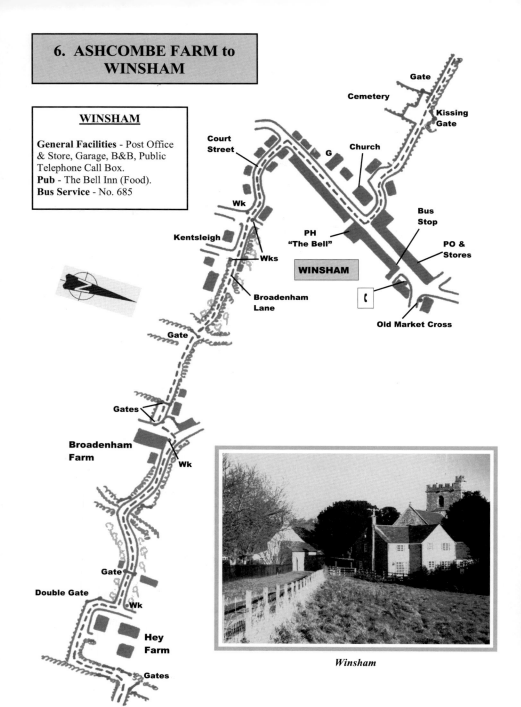

6. ASHCOMBE FARM to WINSHAM

WINSHAM

General Facilities - Post Office & Store, Garage, B&B, Public Telephone Call Box.
Pub - The Bell Inn (Food).
Bus Service - No. 685

Gate

Cemetery

Kissing Gate

Court Street

G

Church

Wk

Bus Stop

Kentsleigh

PH "The Bell"

PO & Stores

Wks

WINSHAM

Broadenham Lane

Old Market Cross

Gate

Gates

Broadenham Farm

Wk

Gate

Double Gate

Wk

Hey Farm

Gates

Winsham

⬤ At the top of the hill the surfaced road becomes a track. Continue on this around the front of 'Hey Farm' where it becomes a surfaced road once again. After passing the farm turn left down the road through an avenue of trees. Carry on down this road passing through a metal gate by some bungalows. This continues to drop down through the avenue of trees to a stream and then climbs uphill again to 'Broadenham Farm'. Turn left at a waymark (Wayford, Winsham), which is beside the stone barn on your left, into a yard and go through the gate ahead of you onto a grass track (waymarked) in front of the farmhouse. Then carry on to a gate into a field keeping the fence and a bungalow on your right. Continue down the field keeping to the right-hand edge until you come to a gap in the corner of the field. Go through the gap and straight across a made up track into a narrow enclosed green lane ('Broadenham Lane'), which eventually leads to a surfaced road. At the bend by some cottages, bear right onto 'Court Street', and continue up to the junction with the main road (B3162) by 'Court Farm House'. You are now in Winsham. Cross the road and turn right on 'Church Street' and go up the road until opposite the 'Bell Inn'. Here turn left into 'Pooles Lane'.

Winsham

Winsham is mentioned in the Domesday Book (1086) as 'Winesha'. 'Winsham' is undoubtedly of Anglo Saxon origin, 'ham' indicating a dwelling place. Today Winsham is a thriving village on the right bank of the Axe close to the Dorset border. The principal street leads up from the river, terminating in an old market cross. The village still retains a shop, pub and the church of St Stephen's. The church, built of flint, has a 'scratch dial'. Above the roof loft there is a wooden board decorated with a Fifteenth Century painting. These pictures are only found in a few churches and Winsham's is unique because it shows the 'Crucifixion' rather than the usual 'Last Judgement' scene. Like many places Winsham once thrived on the woollen cloth industry until the trade went to the north of England.

The Old Market Cross, Winsham

Note:- *Before setting off from Winsham, you should bear in mind that unless you plan to visit Forde Abbey and its tea room is open, there are no further facilities for walkers until you reach Chard Junction* ***(approximately 2¾ miles)***

⬤ Follow the road around behind the church and take the wide footpath with post and rail fencing on one side and iron railings on the other. Follow this path as far as the cemetery.

7. WINSHAM to FORDE ABBEY

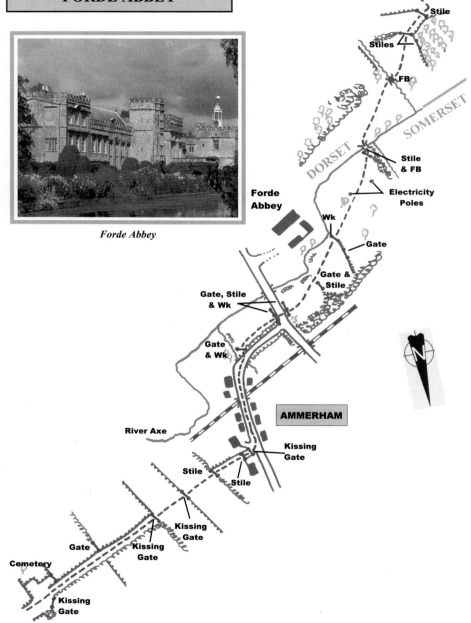

Forde Abbey

Stile

Stiles

FB

DORSET

SOMERSET

Stile & FB

Electricity Poles

Forde Abbey

Wk

Gate

Gate & Stile

Gate, Stile & Wk

Gate & Wk

AMMERHAM

River Axe

N

Kissing Gate

Stile

Stile

Kissing Gate

Gate

Kissing Gate

Kissing Gate

Cemetery

Kissing Gate

⊘ As you pass alongside the cemetery go straight ahead to the narrow path to the right of a metal gate. The path now has a post and wire fence on your left and a hedge on the right. **Follow the path through two fields. At the second field boundary go through a kissing gate and head straight across the field to another kissing gate. Immediately after going through this gate the footpath splits. You take the path straight ahead across the field to a waymarked stile. Cross over and keeping the fence on your left you will come to a stile and, immediately after, a metal kissing gate** (notice how this gate works) **which leads on to the road at Ammerham. Here turn left down the road and over the railway bridge. Just after crossing a stone bridge over a stream go through a gate on your left** (signposted 'Forde Abbey'). **Keep the hedge on your right until you come to a stile which you go over and back on to the road.** (If you wish to visit Forde Abbey turn left along the road. The entrance is about a hundred and fifty yards further along on the right).

Forde Abbey and Gardens

Forde Abbey was founded as a Cistercian Monastery in 1148 and was 'modernised' in 1500 by Abbot Chard. In 1640 the Abbey was turned into a Country House by Edmund Prideaux, who was Cromwell's Attorney General. The magnificent interior is untouched and includes a series of unique plaster ceilings and an outstanding set of Raphael Tapestries which were presented to Sir Frances Gwyn by Queen Anne for services rendered as her secretary of war. Early in the 19th Century the house was rented by Jeremy Bentham the philosopher. Today the Abbey, surrounded by it's 30 acres of gardens and lakes on the bank of the River Axe, is the home of the Roper family. The gardens, which provide a graceful setting for the Abbey, were mostly laid out in the early eighteenth century. The magnificent bog garden was created in 1906 and the walled kitchen garden supplies food for both the present household's needs and the Restaurant. Both the Abbey and the Gardens are well worth a visit. *Gardens open throughout the year, but the Abbey is only open on certain days in the summer. Light lunches and teas served April - October. Check opening times on 01460 221290*

⊘ To continue the walk **go straight across the road to the gate and stile** (signposted River Axe - ½ mile). **Follow the footpath across the middle of the fields to a gate and stile. Go into the next field, and then keeping left, go around to a small waymarked gap to the left of a field gate.** The large building you can see on your left is Forde Abbey. **Go through the gap and head across the field towards two electricity poles, and then carry straight on to a stile and footbridge which spans the river. Cross the bridge** (you are now back in Dorset) **and immediately turn right and head towards the end of the bank of trees on your left** (in the general direction of a solitary cedar tree). **At the end of a wire fence go over a footbridge spanning a small ditch and head uphill to a stile at the end of the copse opposite.**

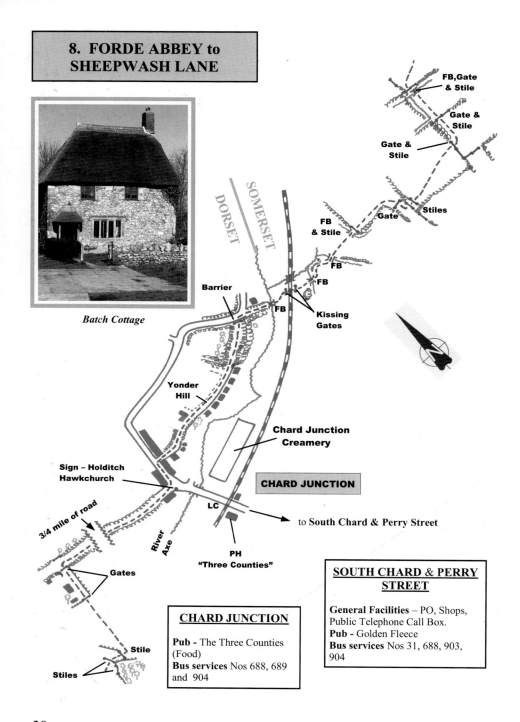

8. FORDE ABBEY to SHEEPWASH LANE

Batch Cottage

FB,Gate & Stile

Gate & Stile

Gate & Stile

Stiles

Gate

DORSET

SOMERSET

FB & Stile

FB

FB

Barrier

FB

Kissing Gates

Yonder Hill

Chard Junction Creamery

CHARD JUNCTION

Sign – Holditch Hawkchurch

3/4 mile of road

LC

River Axe

to **South Chard & Perry Street**

PH "Three Counties"

Gates

Stile

Stiles

CHARD JUNCTION

Pub - The Three Counties (Food)
Bus services Nos 688, 689 and 904

SOUTH CHARD & PERRY STREET

General Facilities – PO, Shops, Public Telephone Call Box.
Pub - Golden Fleece
Bus services Nos 31, 688, 903, 904

28

⬤ **As you get nearer the copse you will see two stiles.** Do not cross over the stile to the right, which leads into the copse itself. **Cross the left-hand stile and go towards the next stile in the post and wire fence. Immediately after going over this turn left following the line of an old field boundary,** which, although removed, is still evident on the ground. **Follow this line up the field aiming towards the wooden building. Eventually the boundary becomes a gravel track as you then go through a metal gate and continue on past some old caravans and a shed. You then go through a wooden gate and onto the road.** When you reach the road you now leave the 'Liberty Trail' which continues on across the road. **Turn right along the road** towards Chard Junction. **Follow the road downhill for about three quarters of a mile until just before the river bridge where you come to a junction opposite 'Chard Creamery'.** You are now at Chard Junction.

Note:- Before continuing from here, you should bear in mind that unless you plan to deviate from the route after about 1¾ miles to visit Tytherleigh, there are no further facilities for walkers until you reach Axminster **(approximately 6¼ miles)**

⬤ To continue the walk, **turn left here** (signposted Holditch, Hawkchurch) **and after about a hundred yards,** just after the first pair of houses, **turn right onto an unsigned footpath** before the next pair of houses. **Follow this as it becomes a footpath with a hedge on the left and the boundary fence of the Creamery on the right. Go uphill** (the river can be seen down on the right) **until at the top, just after a brick building** on the left, **the footpath joins an unmade road.** This is 'Yonder Hill'. **Keep the private residences to your right until the road bears left by 'The Hollies'.** Just before this point notice the lovely 'Batch Cottage' (dated 1684) on your right. **Here go straight across on a wide grass area in front of the holly hedge** which gives the house it's name. **At the end of the hedge the grass area becomes a track surrounded by scrub. Continue on** (do not stray from the path - this is an old quarry working) **until you come to a metal single pole barrier and a road. Turn right and then bear immediately right to go down a lane towards the river again. Cross the footbridge over the river,** leaving Dorset for the last time, **and keeping the river on your left aim for the kissing gate** (waymarked) **across the field alongside the railway bridge. Go through the gate and up the embankment to the railway track. 'STOP, LOOK and LISTEN' before crossing the railway** (there are no footboards!) **and going down to the kissing gate on the other side. Head slightly left to the concrete footbridge over a stream and then follow the stream left to another small bridge. Go over and take the footpath slightly left and uphill to a plank footbridge and stile. Go over the stile and continue to keep the hedge on your right to the end of the field. Here turn right through the metal gate and then immediately left over two stiles in the hedge. Head uphill across the field aiming for the mid-point of the field boundary at the top to a stile and metal gate which are alongside each other. Cross over the stile into a type of lane and immediately turn left and straight on to another stile and gate. Cross the next field keeping the hedge on your left until you get to a stream.**

29

9. SHEEPWASH LANE to COUNTY BOUNDARY

TYTHERLEIGH

Pub - The Tytherleigh Arms (Food and B&B).
Bus Services - Nos. 31, 688, 903 and 904

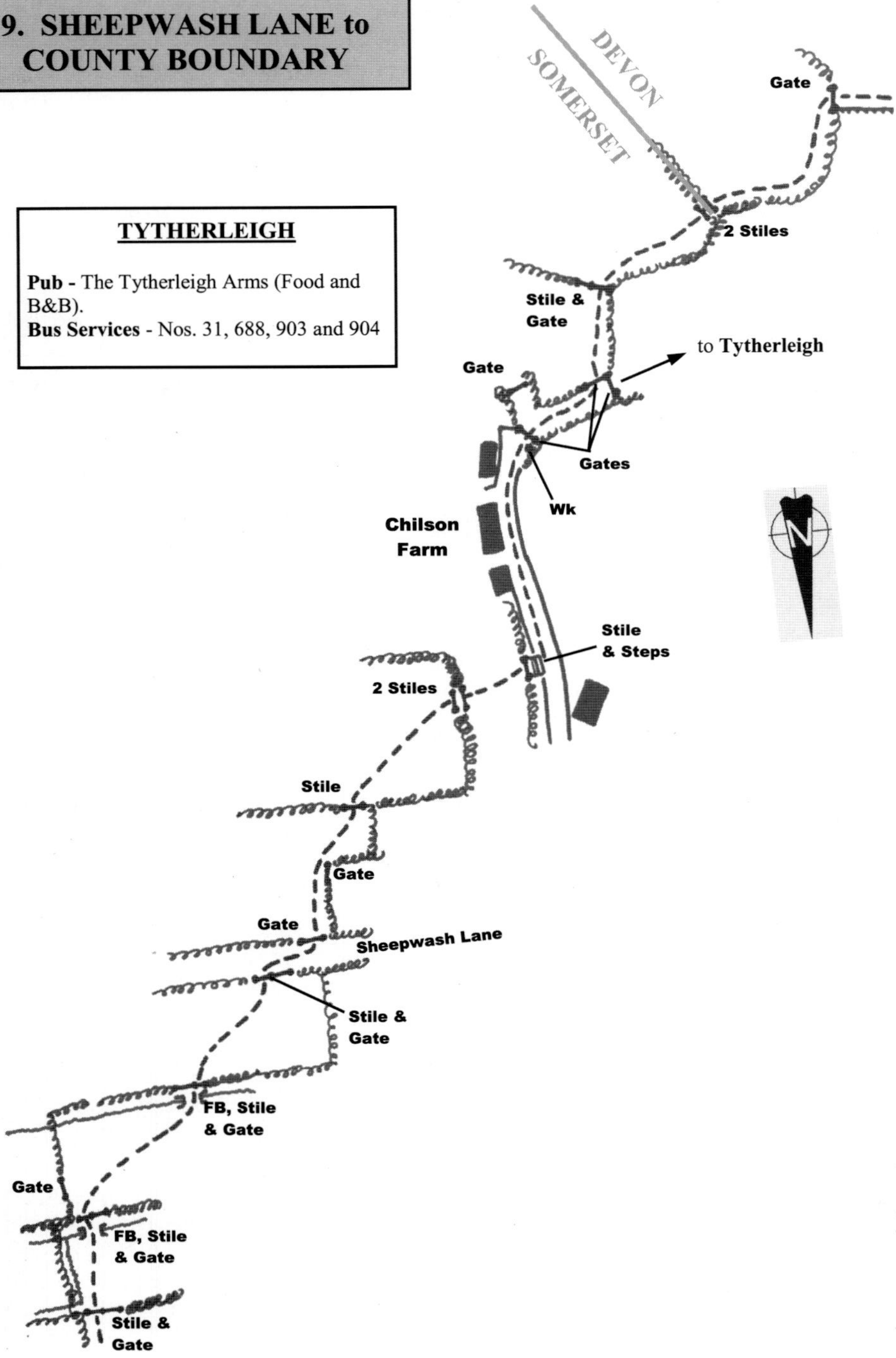

DEVON
SOMERSET

Gate

2 Stiles

Stile & Gate

Gate

to **Tytherleigh**

Gates

Wk

Chilson Farm

N

Stile & Steps

2 Stiles

Stile

Gate

Gate

Sheepwash Lane

Stile & Gate

FB, Stile & Gate

Gate

FB, Stile & Gate

Stile & Gate

⚫ Cross the stream on a plank footbridge to another stile. Go over the stile and head diagonally right across the next field to a plank footbridge and stile alongside a gate. Cross these and head for the opposite right-hand corner of the field to a metal gate and stile. Crossing this stile brings you into a wide green lane, 'Sheepwash Lane'.

Sheepwash Lane

Turn right, and go up the lane a very short distance, and then take the metal gate on your left into the field. Keep to the right-hand edge and where this ends head diagonally right to stile in the hedge. Go into the next field and then go right, aiming towards a point mid-way between the barn and a house, **to a stile. Go over the two stiles in the hedge and cross the narrow field to a stile and carefully down two steps into the lane. Turn left down the lane passing 'Chilson Farm' on your left. Carry on until the lane bears right at a cottage to a wooden gate and waymark** (Tytherleigh Green - ½ mile). **Go through the gate and up to the two metal gates** which form a dead end to the track. The gate straight in front of you leads to Tytherleigh via a public footpath. Although half a mile away off the route Tytherleigh provides a welcome refreshment stop if needed.

Note:- If you do not wish to make this detour now, you can continue your walk to 'Broom Lane', where there is another opportunity to go to Tytherleigh. Otherwise, refreshments etc, will not be available on the route until you reach Axminster, (approximately 4½ miles)

⚫ To continue the walk, **take the left-hand gate** (waymarked) **into the field and then keeping close to the right-hand edge go to a gate and stile in the hedge. Go through and follow the right-hand edge to a double stile. Cross these** (as you cross the second of these stiles, you will have entered Devon) **and keep to the right-hand edge to a wooden gate.**

31

*The Letterbox at
Flintstone Cottage*

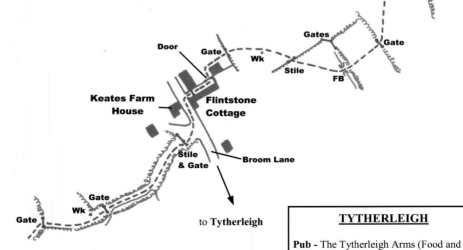

to **Tytherleigh**

⬤ Go through the gate into the next field and follow a post and wire fence on the right straight down to a waymark followed by a metal gate in the corner. **This leads into an enclosed lane** which also serves for part of the way as a stream, and subsequently is very wet, especially in winter. **Follow the lane all the way up to a gate and stile at 'Keates Farm' and eventually to the lane's junction with another surfaced road,** 'Broom Lane'. (If you now wish to get refreshments at Tytherleigh you should turn right and go up the lane for about a third of a mile). **For the walk turn left and go down the road passing 'Keates Farm House'** on the left. **When you come to 'Flintstone Cottage',** on the right, look out for it's delightful letterbox. This letterbox serves as a useful guide because, **immediately on your right, the footpath is signposted through the yard of the cottage.** It is easy to miss this sign in the direction you are going. **Go through the yard via a metal gate and then through the doorway on your left** (waymarked). **This takes you into a garden where you should go right, around some garages, and down to a garden gate** (waymarked). **Go across the field bearing slightly right**

Keates Farm House and Broom Lane

and follow the waymarks to a stile in the post and wire fence. Go over the stile and then turn left across the field to a point about twenty yards up from two metal gates. Here you need to cross a stream by means of a sleeper footbridge. You then go through the gap in the hedge into the next field. Go straight ahead to a metal gate and into the next field. You now go slightly left downhill to yet another metal gate which you will not see until you get to the brow of the hill. **Go through the gate and then turn immediately left and head down the left-hand edge of the field. Keep following this left-hand edge passing through a metal gate until eventually reaching a concrete farm track. Turn right onto the track and follow this down towards 'Axe Farm' until just before a metal gate.** Do not go through the gate, but instead **turn off right into the field.**

33

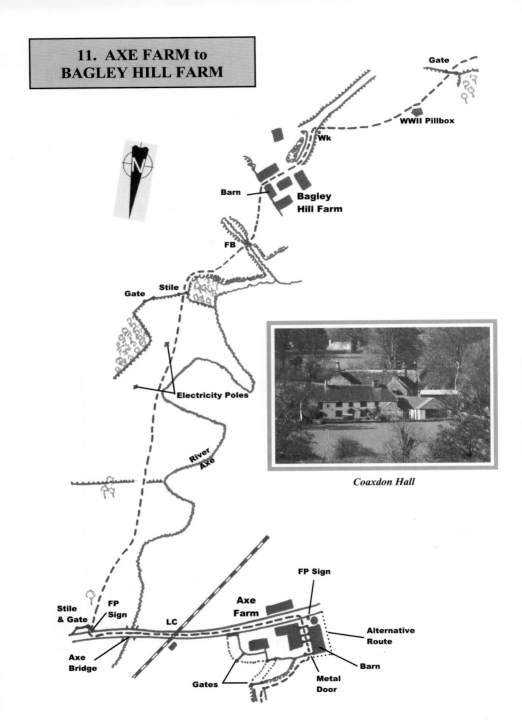

11. AXE FARM to BAGLEY HILL FARM

Gate

WWII Pillbox

Wk

Barn

Bagley Hill Farm

N

FB

Gate   Stile

Electricity Poles

River Axe

Coaxdon Hall

FP Sign

Axe Farm

Stile & Gate

FP Sign

LC

Alternative Route

Axe Bridge

Gates

Metal Door

Barn

⊗ **When in the field keep the hedge on your left and just before the barn turn left into the farmyard, via the metal door.** (If there is livestock in the farmyard carry on past the barn and turn left through the metal gate instead). **Go through the farmyard** (or the field) **and out onto the road. At the road, turn left, and continue on to a level crossing** which has automatic barriers. **A few yards further along the road, after crossing the railway, you will come to 'Axe Bridge'. After crossing the river you arrive at a footpath sign on your right by a stile and metal gate. Go over the stile into the field and head straight ahead aiming for a bend in the river. When you reach this, carry on, aiming to the right of an old tree, to a gap in the fence. Go straight ahead heading for another bend in the river in a general direction of about fifty yards to the right of an electricity pole. When close to the river head off away for a stile in the fence ahead by the edge of a clump of trees. Cross the stile and head right across the next field to a footbridge. Cross the waymarked bridge and head diagonally left, uphill, to a point between the farmhouse and a barn.** This is 'Bagley Hill Farm'. **Go through the farmyard and up a concrete road. At the top of the slope by a waymark, go right into the field and then head diagonally left downhill towards an old World War II pillbox.** When you reach the pillbox look across the river to your right and to the other side of the railway. You will see 'Coaxdon Hall'. It was here that Charles II sought refuge from his pursuers following the battle of Worcester, a feat he reputedly achieved by hiding under the petticoat of the lady of the house, a Mrs Cogan! As a reward she received a gold chain and locket bearing his arms.

The Axe near Axe Farm

35

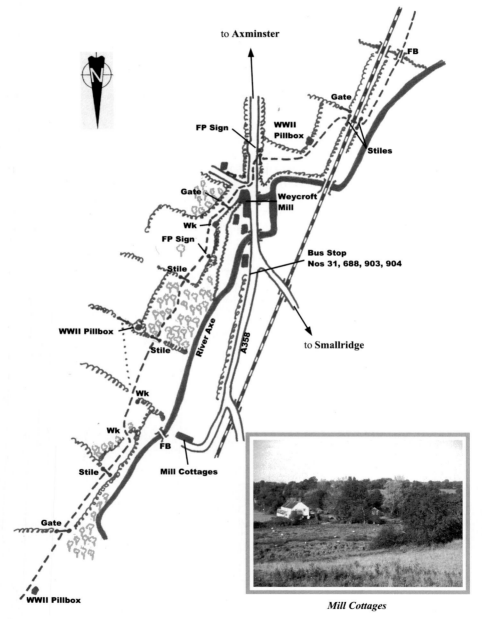

to **Axminster**

FB

FP Sign

Gate

WWII
Pillbox

Stiles

Gate

Weycroft
Mill

Wk

FP Sign

Bus Stop
Nos 31, 688, 903, 904

Stile

WWII Pillbox

River Axe

A358

to **Smallridge**

Stile

Wk

Wk

FB

Mill Cottages

Stile

Gate

WWII Pillbox

Mill Cottages

⬅ **Carry on straight ahead and downhill towards a metal gate, which is on the left-hand edge of a small coppice. Go through and follow the right-hand field edge to a stile. Go over this and then head slightly left to a waymarked gap in the trees opposite. Head diagonally uphill away from the river to a waymark in the hedge where the overhead power lines cross. Now go straight ahead towards a coppice,** <u>not</u> diagonally left and uphill on a more obvious path to the gate you see on the skyline. Notice the old Mill Cottages down by the river to your right. **As you near the coppice you will see a waymarked stile. Go over this and into the coppice continuing on until you come to another stile at the far end. Go over this into the field and follow the right-hand side of the field edge, with trees on your right, to a footpath sign pointing the way you have just come. From here head slightly right downhill to a waymark by another World War II pillbox. At the waymark go down the track by the mill leat of 'Weycroft Mill' to a metal gate. Go through the gate and continue on to the road junction** ('Lodge Lane'). It is thought that there has been a mill on this site since Domesday. The present mill was still milling flour on a commercial basis up until 1965 and was eventually closed in the early 1970's. If you go left up Lodge Lane you will come to the 'Manor House' which was the site of 'Weycroft Hall'. This was an early fifteenth century building licensed in 1417 to have its own private chapel. The most interesting remaining feature is the Great Hall which runs for the full height of the house. **To continue the walk turn right and go down to the main road** (A358). If you turn right at the main road you will come to 'Weycroft Bridge' or 'Stratford Bridge' as it was once called. The name 'Stratford' derives from the Old English for a paved ford carrying a Roman road which in this case was the 'Fosse Way'. **At the main road turn left and, just before the lay-by on the left, cross the road and go through the metal field gate** (signposted footpath) **on the other side and into the field. Head across the field towards the jutting out corner of the hedge and yet another World War II pillbox. Go past this and head downhill to the metal gate and stile you will see alongside the railway. Go over the stile and 'STOP, LOOK and LISTEN' before crossing the railway** (beware, there are no footboards on the track!). **Go over the stile on the far side. Go a few yards ahead and then left along the top of a low flood mound. Follow this alongside the railway until you come to a footbridge across a drainage stream. Cross this and continue on towards the road bridge you will see in the distance.** Over on the hill to your right you can see Cloakham House.

Cloakham House and Bridge

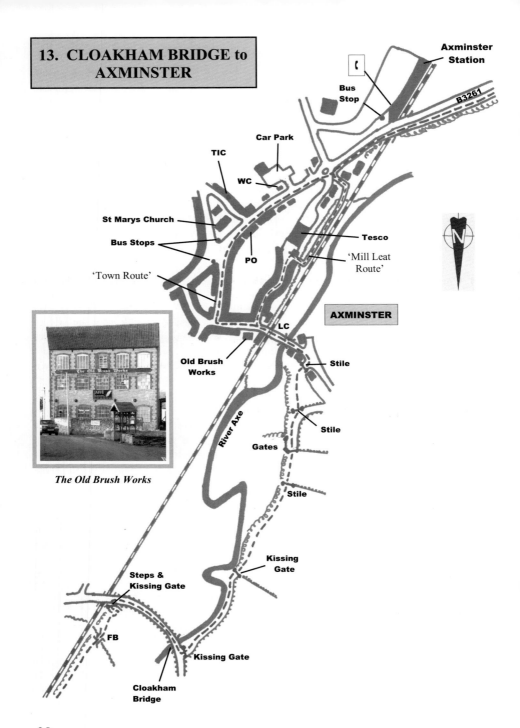

13. CLOAKHAM BRIDGE to AXMINSTER

Axminster Station

Bus Stop

B3261

Car Park

TIC

WC

St Marys Church

Bus Stops

'Town Route'

PO

Tesco

'Mill Leat Route'

AXMINSTER

LC

Old Brush Works

Stile

Stile

River Axe

Gates

Stile

The Old Brush Works

Kissing Gate

Steps & Kissing Gate

FB

Kissing Gate

Cloakham Bridge

⬤ **After crossing another stream, carry on towards the bridge and climb the steps up onto the road, turning right at the top. Go down the road as far as the river bridge.** This is Cloakham Bridge, a delightful single span stone arched bridge. **After crossing this take the footpath immediately signed to the left through a kissing gate. The footpath now keeps the river on your left and a post and wire fence on your right. Follow the river to the point where it seems to almost meet itself. Go right through a metal kissing gate into a field. Continue along the left-hand side with a hedge on your left to a stile. Go over the stile and continue to keep the hedge on your left to a metal gate. Go through and straight ahead and then just after the track becomes concreted and the hedge ends, go left over a stile in a wire fence. Cross the field to the far side to a stile between two houses leading on to the road. Turn left and go over 'Stoney Bridge' and then the level crossing** which has

Cloakham Bridge

automatic barriers. Note 'Ducking Stool Bridge' on your right and the old Brush Works on your left. Just past the Brush Works is the 'Green Dragon House', where, having to flee from the soldiers of James I because he had supported Monmouth, Robert Cogan is supposed to have hidden in the bed of the landlady's daughter. Credibility is given to this story by the fact that Cogan did in fact marry her.

*There is now a choice of two routes. Either the **'Town' Route,** which is the slightly longer of the two, takes you into the centre of Axminster, giving you an opportunity to look around the town itself. Or alternatively, the **'Mill Leat' Route** which avoids the town centre altogether.*

The 'Mill Leat' Route

⬤ **Just after passing the Brush Works turn right into 'Vale Lane' and continue on to what will appear to be a dead end.** At the end you will see a footpath to your right (signed - Public Footpath to Station via Vale Lane). **Go along here, over the mill leat, and continue along the path between the leat and the railway. After crossing back over the leat once more continue on until you have to turn left and you rejoin the 'Town' route just past the roundabout. Turn right and go up to the railway bridge.**

39

The 'Town' Route

⬆ **After passing the Brush Works and the 'Green Dragon' continue up the hill before turning right into 'Castle Street'. Continue uphill,** noting the 'Old Clink' door set in the wall on your left, **until you arrive at 'Trinity Square'** and the centre of Axminster.

The Old Clink

Axminster

Early closing - *Wednesday,* **Market Day** - *Thursday*
General Facilities - *Post Office, Banks, Hotels and B&B's, Shops, Restaurants, Cafes, Library and other such facilities found in a small market town.* **Pubs** - *(all close to the town centre)* - *Axminster Inn, The Castle (Food), Red Lion, Cavalier Inn, Lamb Inn (Food and B&B) and The George Inn (Food and B&B).* **Bus Services** - *Nos. 31, 885, 380, 688, 689, 903 and 904.* **Rail Station** - *to Exeter and London Waterloo.* **Tourist Information Centre** - *has limited opening hours in winter (which at the beginning of 2000 were 10.00 - 13.00hrs on Mondays, Thursdays and Fridays).* **Museum** – *Open in Summer only – contact Axminster TIC (01297 34386) for details.*

The carpets, to which Axminster gives its name, tend to be more widely known than the town itself, however, Axminster is by no means just a carpet town. Although two Roman roads, the 'Fosse Way' and 'Icknield Street', crossed each other less than a mile to the south, the town was not a Roman settlement. Similarly, despite what the street names 'Castle Hill' and 'Castle Street' may suggest, it has been considered unlikely that Axminster ever had a castle. It was, however, one of the earliest Saxon settlements in Devon a church having being founded here just before Cyneheard's death in 786 AD. One of Axminster's last remaining links with the past are at 'Lower Abbey Farm', to the south-west of the town, where now only a few stones mark the site of 'Newenham Abbey', a Cistercian abbey, founded in 1247. It is thought that the stones forming the arched entrance to the 'Archway Bookshop', next to the museum in 'Church Street', originally came from the Abbey. The museum also houses the Tourist Information Centre. Even today Axminster remains a true market town, a weekly market being held on Thursdays for sheep, cattle and pigs. This market, granted by King John, moved from the square to its present home in South Street in 1912 after giving way to a more modern pannier market. Perhaps the most imposing part of Axminster is 'Trinity Square' and the parish church of St Mary's which overlooks it. The square is named after a fire which occurred on Trinity Sunday in 1834, which destroyed twenty four houses and raged as far as the former 'Bell Inn', closed in the early 1980's and since reopened as shops. 'The George Hotel' is an eighteenth century stone built Inn and, as is apparent from the entrance archway, was once a coaching Inn. Situated on the London – Dorchester – Exeter route it once catered for as many as sixteen coaches a day. During the Civil War the inn played host to Cromwell and his men.

Also in the square is a combined drinking fountain and lighting column which was built to mark the Silver Jubilee in 1887. The church of St Mary's stands on the same site as it's predecessor, founded over twelve hundred years earlier, of which nothing now remains. The tower dates from the thirteenth century and is unusually situated in the centre of the church. The carpet in the church is of course an 'Axminster', and is a gift of the company whose world famous carpet production was started in the town by Thomas Whitty in 1755. His original factory was destroyed by fire in 1828 which resulted in an even bigger place being built. Whitty died in 1792, aged eighty, but his high standards were maintained by subsequent generations of the family. The former factory still stands in 'Silver Street' and became the first home of Axminster Hospital in 1886. The hospital moved to Chard Road in 1912. Carpet making returned to Axminster in 1936 but to its present site in 'Woolsmead Road'.

The Jubilee Fountain

The 'Town' Route (continued)

⬤ **From 'Trinity Square' follow 'Anchor Hill' down towards the railway station. At the roundabout go straight across staying on the footpath alongside the B3261,** where the alternative 'Mill Leat' route rejoins from your right, **and continue on up to the railway bridge.**

The main railway came to Axminster in 1860 and survived the infamous 'Beeching Axe' just over a hundred years later. The branch line to Lyme Regis, opened in 1903,

was however less fortunate, and was closed in 1965. The station building, completed in 1859, is typical of many along this rail route, but is one of only a few surviving and still used for it's original purpose. When first built the chimneys were a lot taller than they are now.

Axminster Railway Station

14. AXMINSTER to KILMINGTON

KILMINGTON

General Facilities - Shop, B&B, Public Telephone Call Box. Kilmington Chef (Food), Traveller's Lodge (Acc'm).
Pubs - The Old Inn (Food) and The New Inn (Food).
Bus Services - Nos. 380 and 689.

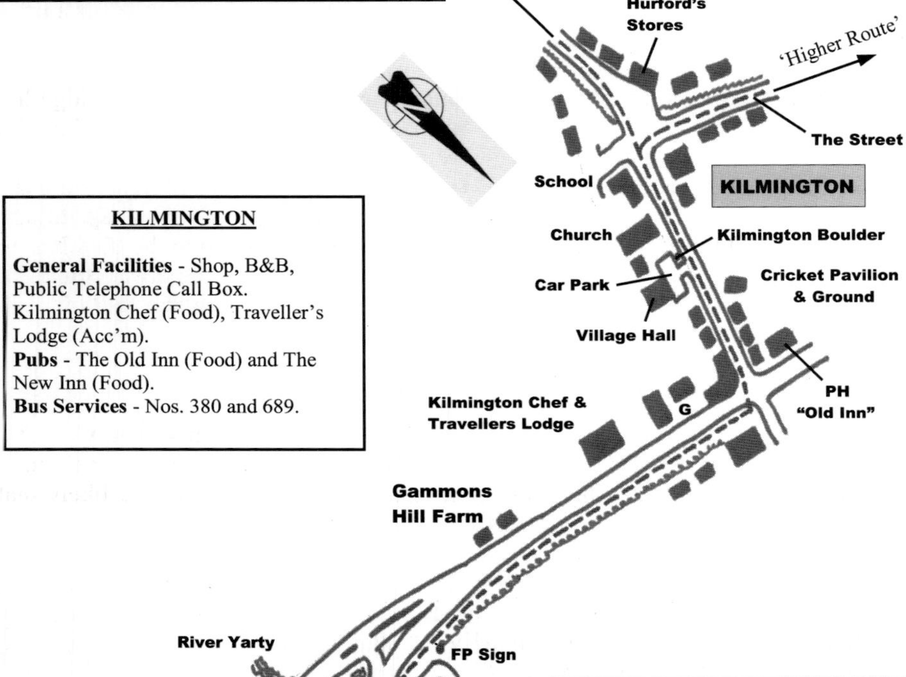

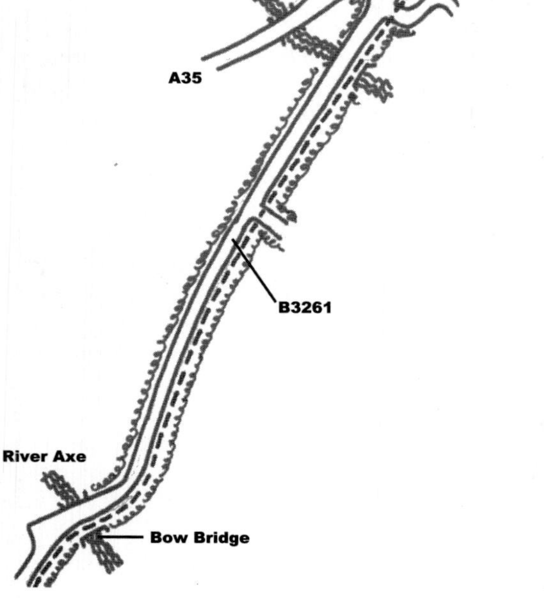

'Lower Route'
Hurford's Stores
'Higher Route'
The Street
KILMINGTON
School
Church
Kilmington Boulder
Car Park
Cricket Pavilion & Ground
Village Hall
PH "Old Inn"
Kilmington Chef & Travellers Lodge
G
Gammons Hill Farm
River Yarty
FP Sign
A35
B3261
River Axe
Bow Bridge

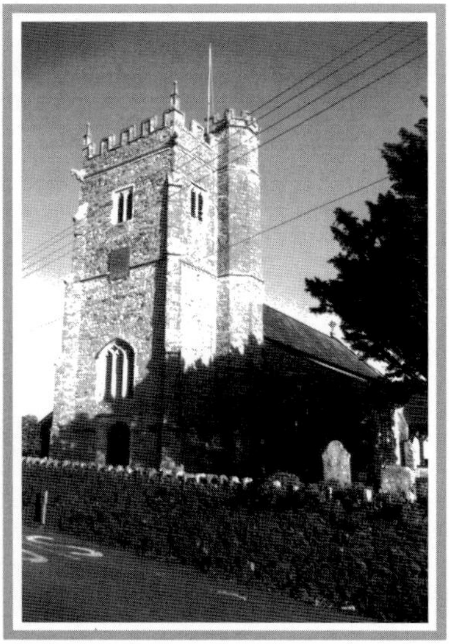

St Gile's Church, Kilmington

⬤ After crossing over the railway bridge continue on the footpath and over first 'Bow Bridge' (The River Axe) and then, after almost a quarter of a mile, over another bridge (The River Yarty). It is almost certain that the Romans would have crossed this same stretch of marshy ground by means of timber decks on timber-trestle piers. Being of such a semi-permanent nature, none of this type of bridge has ever survived. Continue on until you arrive at the road's junction with the A35 Axminster Bypass. Here keep right on the footpath, and follow it up the hill, 'Gammons Hill', towards Kilmington. After passing the filling station on your left cross the road with extreme care and continue the short distance up to the crossroads. At the crossroads go straight across if you wish to go to the 'Old Inn' or the 'New Inn' (which is a quarter of a mile further on up the hill), otherwise turn left into 'Whitford Road'. After about 200 yards you will come to the 'Kilmington Boulder' and the Village Hall on your left.

Kilmington

Although Kilmington lies on the line of a Roman Road, like Axminster it was not a Roman settlement. The centre of the village is to the south of the main road and is referred to in the Domesday book as 'Chienmetona', and it is therefore likely that Kilmington was a very early Saxon settlement. The original translation is thought to be based on 'the home of a man called Coenhelm', which in turn became 'Coenhelmingaston' and eventually 'Kilmington'. The 'new' village hall was opened in 1985 as a result of the local community being faced with having to close their old hall. The old hall now serves as the cricket and bowls pavilion. The 'Kilmington Boulder' was found in the nearby quarry, and, as the inscription tells us, "is probably one hundred million years old". A chronological support of this theory is mounted on the right-hand side of the entrance porch to the hall. The church of St Giles was restored in 1861 - 62, and only the tower remains from the original building.

The Kilmington Boulder

⬤ Continue on along the road, passing the Church of St Giles on your left, and carry on until you reach the school which is on your left.

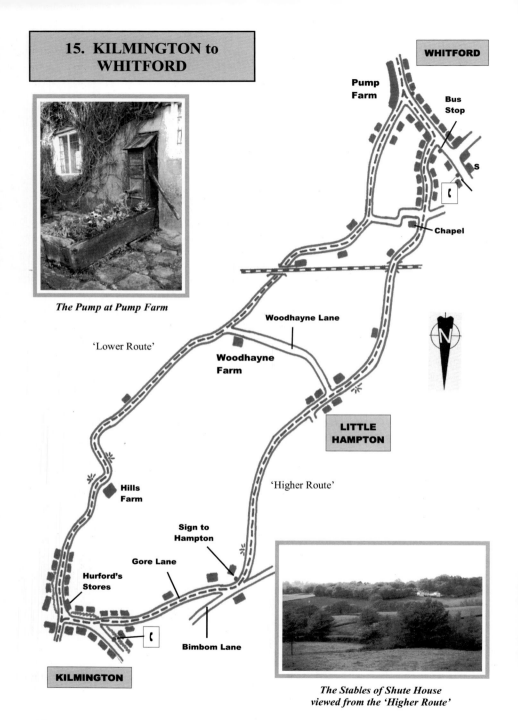

15. KILMINGTON to WHITFORD

The Pump at Pump Farm

WHITFORD

Pump Farm

Bus Stop

S

Chapel

'Lower Route'

Woodhayne Lane

Woodhayne Farm

N

LITTLE HAMPTON

Hills Farm

'Higher Route'

Sign to Hampton

Gore Lane

Hurford's Stores

Bimbom Lane

KILMINGTON

The Stables of Shute House viewed from the 'Higher Route'

44

You have the choice of two routes from Kilmington to Whitford; the 'Lower' Route or a 'Higher' Route via Little Hampton. Both are along roads and both offer superb views of the Axe Valley. The 'Higher' route is quieter from a traffic point of view, but is the slightly longer and more strenuous of the two.

The 'Lower' Route

After passing the school follow the road straight on over the bridge. Follow this road for almost half a mile to 'Hills Farm'. Here stop awhile and take in

The view from Hills Farm with the sea on the horizon

the superb views of the Axe Valley and a far distance glimpse of the sea. **The road now starts to go downhill towards the river and railway. Continue on and, just past 'Woodhayne Lane', go under the railway and continue along the road into Whitford,** where you join the 'Higher' route at 'Pump Farm'.

The 'Higher' Route

Just past the school turn right up 'The Street' until just before a telephone call box. Here go over a bridge on your left into 'Gore Lane'. Carry on up this lane until it is joined by 'Bimbom Lane'. Here bear left into 'Hampton Lane'. Follow the road for about three quarters of a mile and on through 'Little Hampton' and its farms. Notice the collection of old farm machinery at the lower farm and the stables of 'Shute House' on the hill over to your right. **Carry on downhill over the railway bridge and into Whitford. Cross the ford near 'Burts Farm' and at the main road turn left towards the river** (signed Musbury). **Eventually you arrive at a Y junction,** the road from the left being the 'Lower' route from Kilmington described above, **by 'Pump Farm'.**

45

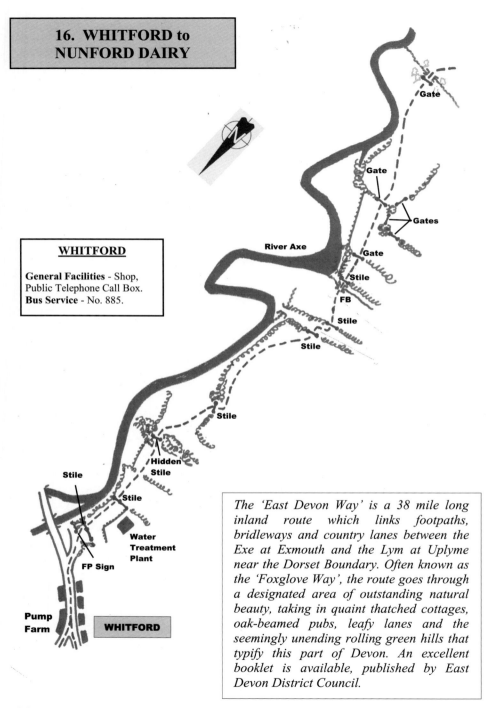

16. WHITFORD to NUNFORD DAIRY

Gate

Gate

Gates

River Axe

Gate

Stile

FB

Stile

Stile

Stile

WHITFORD

General Facilities - Shop, Public Telephone Call Box.
Bus Service - No. 885.

Stile

Hidden Stile

Stile

Stile

Water Treatment Plant

FP Sign

Pump Farm

WHITFORD

The 'East Devon Way' is a 38 mile long inland route which links footpaths, bridleways and country lanes between the Exe at Exmouth and the Lym at Uplyme near the Dorset Boundary. Often known as the 'Foxglove Way', the route goes through a designated area of outstanding natural beauty, taking in quaint thatched cottages, oak-beamed pubs, leafy lanes and the seemingly unending rolling green hills that typify this part of Devon. An excellent booklet is available, published by East Devon District Council.

Pump Farm, Whitford – a fine example of a Devon Longhouse

At 'Pump Farm' continue on the road towards the river (signposted Musbury and Axminster). **Just before reaching the river turn to the right onto a track** which was the road leading to the now demolished old river bridge. **Bearing right,** (signposted footpath) **go over a stile and onto a track alongside a water treatment works. At the end of the works go over another stile and into a field, following its left-hand side aiming for the gap in the hedge opposite. After passing through this gap into the next field bear downhill to the far left-hand corner where hidden from previous view you will find a stile. Cross the stile in the hedge and carry on straight ahead on a faintly discernible footpath for about 50 yards until you are opposite a stile in the hedge on your right. Go towards and cross the stile, turn left and keep close to the left-hand hedge and the river. Where the hedge peters out head for an obvious stile in the middle of the hedge on the far side. Cross this into a lane.** The path you are now on is part of the 'East Devon Way' (see notes on opposite page) which you will now follow as far as Colyford. (If you turn left it will take you to Musbury). **However to continue the walk you have to turn right and, after going along the lane for about 20 yards, go left over a stile into a field. Continue across the field to a plank footbridge and another stile. Keep the hedge and trees on your left and go through the gate into the next field. Head straight ahead to a corner of the hedge that juts out. Carry on, keeping this on your right, to a metal gate. Go through and head straight across the field back towards the river again. As you come close to a bend in the river carry on straight ahead to a gate and field access bridge over a stream.**

47

17. NUNFORD DAIRY to COLYFORD

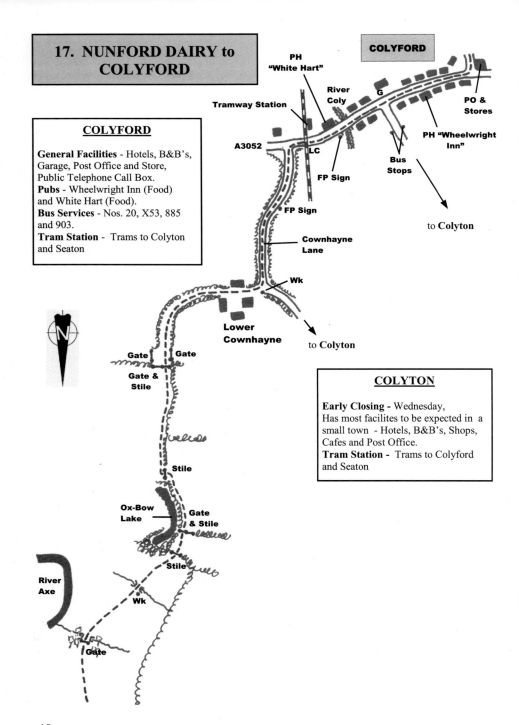

COLYFORD

COLYFORD

General Facilities - Hotels, B&B's, Garage, Post Office and Store, Public Telephone Call Box.
Pubs - Wheelwright Inn (Food) and White Hart (Food).
Bus Services - Nos. 20, X53, 885 and 903.
Tram Station - Trams to Colyton and Seaton

PH "White Hart"

River Coly

G

PO & Stores

Tramway Station

A3052

LC

FP Sign

Bus Stops

PH "Wheelwright Inn"

to **Colyton**

FP Sign

Cownhayne Lane

Wk

Lower Cownhayne

to **Colyton**

COLYTON

Early Closing - Wednesday, Has most facilites to be expected in a small town - Hotels, B&B's, Shops, Cafes and Post Office.
Tram Station - Trams to Colyford and Seaton

Gate

Gate

Gate & Stile

Stile

Ox-Bow Lake

Gate & Stile

Stile

River Axe

Wk

Gate

⬤ Go over the bridge into the next field and continue slightly right across the field, heading towards a tall waymark, which is alongside a bridge over a stream. From the waymark continue towards the right-hand corner of the field and another stile. Go over this and turn left along the field boundary and pass a swampy pond (an old Ox-Bow lake) on your left. Go straight ahead towards a stile and gate. Go over the stile and follow the left-hand edge to another stile on the left. Cross this and turn immediately right, keeping the hedge on your right. Follow the hedge around (crossing a plank footbridge on the way) to a wooden gate and stile leading to a track to 'Lower Cownhayne'. Follow this track through the farm to its junction with a metalled lane ('Cownhayne Lane'). If you wish to visit Colyton (see notes below) you can turn right here; the town centre is about a mile away. However for the walk turn left (waymarked EDW) and follow the lane for almost half a mile to the main road (A3052) at Colyford.

Colyton

Although off the main walking route, Colyton is only a mile from either 'Lower Cownhayne', which you have just passed, or Colyford. Colyton is a unique little market town with almost all the buildings lining the labyrinth of streets being centuries old. With many of the shops still retaining traditional family run businesses there is so much of interest for the visitor to see all packed into a relatively small area.

There are two ways of walking the final couple of miles or so into Seaton. The B3172 via Axmouth is a very busy road with no footpath for much of the way. Therefore for the purpose of completing the walking notes we have chosen to describe the route below, as it is along a less busy road. Consequently, depending on whether or not it is in operation at the time, we would strongly recommend using the 'Seaton Tramway' to complete your journey. However for the purists who wish to complete the whole walk on foot, walking the described route will also give you the opportunity to visit the Seaton Marshes Local Nature Reserve if it is open. (see notes on page 51)

⬤ Turn right along the A3052 and over the level crossing. If you wish to catch a tram turn left immediately after the level crossing. Carry on over the bridge spanning the River Coly and continue up Swan Hill. Note the old petrol pumps in the garage on your left. It was here that Lawrence of Arabia frequently stopped for petrol, and indeed is reputed to have stopped here on the day he met his death. The garage still maintains the tradition of attendant service. Continue uphill as far as the Post Office.

The 'old style' petrol pumps at Colyford

18. COLYFORD to SEATON (and AXMOUTH)

SEATON

Market Day - Monday.
General Facilities - has all the facilities normally found in a small seaside resort.
Pubs - Hook & Parrot (Food), The Famous George (Food), Fishermans Inn (Food and B&B), Eyre Court Hotel (Food and B&B), Kings Arms (Food), JD's.
Bus Services - Nos. 20, 378, X53, 885, 899 and 903.
Tram Station - Trams to Colyford and Colyton.

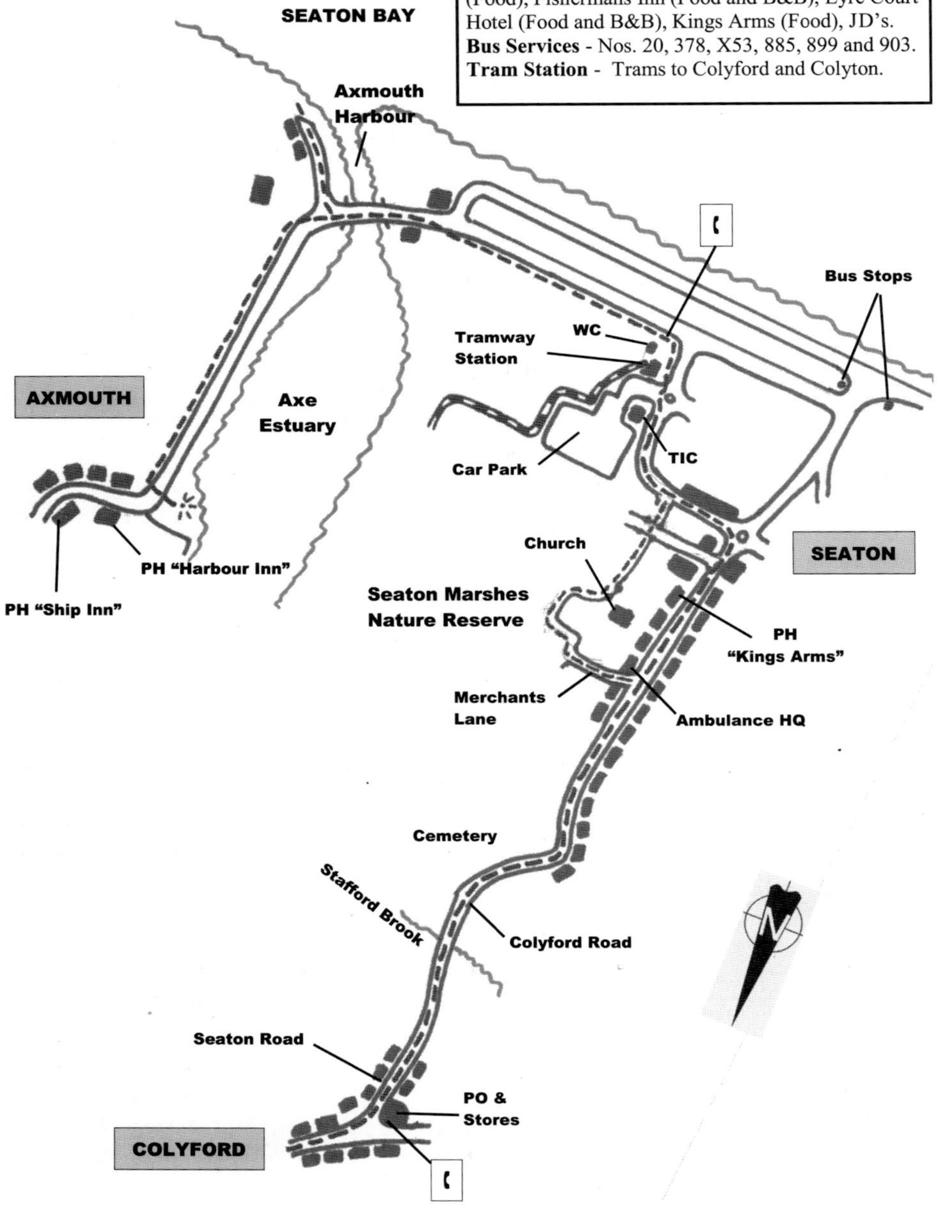

SEATON BAY

Axmouth Harbour

Bus Stops

Tramway Station

WC

AXMOUTH

Axe Estuary

Car Park

TIC

PH "Harbour Inn"

Church

SEATON

PH "Ship Inn"

Seaton Marshes Nature Reserve

PH "Kings Arms"

Merchants Lane

Ambulance HQ

Cemetery

Stafford Brook

Colyford Road

Seaton Road

PO & Stores

COLYFORD

Colyford

Colyford consists of character properties which straddle a long main street, which is the busy A3052. Originally this formed part of the old Roman route from Dorchester to Exeter. It was set up as a borough by Thomas Basset in the early part of the 13th century and, to this day, still elects a mayor. Colyford was also the birthplace of Sir Thomas Gates who was Governor of Virginia from 1611 to 1614. Although it is difficult to visualise now Colyford was once an important port, but the draining of the Axe Marshes from about 1660 onwards led to the eventual demise of this function. Today Colyford is well served by other forms of transport including the famous Seaton Tramway.

When you come to the Post Office turn left down 'Seaton Road' and follow this road towards Seaton. The bridge over what is Stafford Brook marks the parish boundary, and the point where 'Seaton Road' becomes 'Colyford Road'. **Continue to follow the road,** passing the Cemetery on your left, **until you reach the St John Ambulance Headquarters** on your left.

As we went to print the Seaton Marshes Local Nature Reserve was at an advanced stage of being opened up to the public. Should the Reserve not be open, or if you wish to go directly to the town centre and seafront, continue the walk from the top of the next page.

Seaton Marshes Local Nature Reserve

This Local Nature Reserve consists of about 25 acres of marshland. Here grazing will continue along traditional lines and existing ditches carefully managed. As a result, the number and type of aquatic plants and invertebrates will be increased which in turn will attract other forms of wildlife. Future plans include the creation of a new pond, lagoon and a bird hide. The whole project has involved the co-operation of East Devon District Council, The Axe Vale and District Conservation Society and South West Water. Eventually it is hoped that, with the collaboration of Seaton Tramway, organised birdwatching trips can also be promoted. The reserve will provide pleasure for local people and visitors alike, as well as becoming a valuable educational resource. *Telephone 01395 516551 for further details.*

To visit the Reserve **turn left into 'Merchant's Lane' and follow this down to the entrance to the Reserve.** The route through the Reserve will be signposted but note that part of the route will be a permissive path only and that no dogs will be allowed. **From the Reserve follow the footpath alongside the right-hand edge of the marshes. After passing St Gregory's Parish Church** on your right **continue on the footpath to a kissing gate. Go through this and straight across the track** (Clapps Lane) **and continue on the footpath to the road,** 'The Underfleet', where you rejoin the main route.

For the main route, continue straight on along Colyford Road until you eventually reach a roundabout. The town centre and seafront are now straight ahead along 'Fore Street'. **For the walk turn left at the roundabout into 'The Underfleet' and along the footpath** where just before the play park the Nature Reserve route joins from your left. **Continue along the footpath** passing a car park on your left **until you reach a roundabout.** Turn left here for the Tramway Station and Tourist Information Centre.

A Seaton Tram

Seaton Tramway

The Seaton Tramway is a narrow (2ft 9ins) gauge tramway affording the opportunity of a three mile journey alongside the beautiful Axe Estuary, viewing its wildlife on the way. It also offers an environmentally friendly and relaxing way of visiting Colyton, Colyford and Seaton. Purpose built and lovingly restored tramcars, including open topped and enclosed versions, ensure a comfortable ride whatever the weather. The trams themselves are roughly half the size of the old town trams that use to run in Britain before World War II. The complete return journey takes about one hour. *The Tramway is normally open from April to November and holds several special event days throughout the year. Telephone 01297 20375 for timetables etc.*

Seaton

Located to the west of the Axe, where it finally flows into the sea after it's 24 mile long journey, Seaton is a holiday resort enjoying the relative shelter of Lyme Bay. It lies between the striking red marl of Haven Cliffs to the west, and the white chalk cliffs of Beer Head to the east. A long pebble beach runs in front of the 'Esplanade' with a more secluded beach situated to the east of Axmouth Harbour. Most of the older buildings are of Victorian and Edwardian origin. The town centre itself is now pedestrianised, allowing carefree shopping in the many small and varied shops. The Axe Valley Heritage Museum is situated on the top floor of the Town Hall in Fore Street, and houses many documents and photographs depicting times gone by. *Open Mon – Fri from May to October, admission free. Telephone 01297 21278 for details.*

Continue the walk by going straight on from the roundabout when you will immediately come to another at which you turn left into Harbour Road. Follow this road all the way to the two bridges that span the Axe.

Axmouth Bridge

The old bridge was completed in 1877 and is thought to be the oldest surviving 'all concrete' bridge in the country. Before the bridge was built there was a ferry crossing the Axe and it was not until the early 1870's that Philip Brannon was engaged to build a concrete bridge to replace it. Brannon, in his design, completely misjudged the strength of the ground on which the bridge foundations were built. This resulted in the western pier settling some two feet into the river bed even before the bridge was opened to traffic. A plainly visible attempt was made to give

Axmouth Bridge

the outward appearance of a masonry structure. To complement the bridge an all concrete toll house was built on the western side and this was in use until tolls were abolished in 1907. Both the bridge and the toll house are now listed buildings, with the bridge also being a designated ancient monument. Despite being strengthened in 1956, it eventually became necessary to replace the bridge completely and as a result the present 'new' road bridge was constructed alongside.

After crossing the old bridge turn right and go along the road passing the picturesque Harbour master's cottages on the way. Continue on alongside Axmouth Harbour until the road ends. You can now walk the final short distance to the sea and there contemplate - JOURNEY'S END !

Beer Head from the mouth of the Axe

Axmouth

Established in the seventh century, Axmouth is a beautiful village which was once a thriving and important south coast port. It now features some fine examples of 18th and 19th Century farmhouses and cottages. Cottages and even now remains relatively unspoilt. It has become accepted that the 'Fosse Way' ended at Axmouth, based on the assumption that it was once a Roman port. Despite the silting up of the estuary, vessels were still able to unload at a pier built in 1803 and continued to do so even when the railway arrived to Seaton in 1868. However the coming

Axmouth

of the railway eventually led to the final decay of Axmouth as a port, the pier being lost in 1869. The centre of the village is dominated by St Michael's Church which contains work from several periods with substantial remains of Norman origin.

If you wish to visit Axmouth, which will add almost ¾ mile to the overall walk, **from the bridge bear left and follow the footpath alongside the road all the way to the village itself.** This route offers fine views of the Estuary, the marshes and Seaton beyond. You will also pass the entrance to 'Stedcombe House' built in 1691 (not open to the public). **As you approach the village the road bends sharply to the right. On your left is a picnic site alongside the estuary,** which is the perfect spot to sit, relax and enjoy the fine view back down the estuary itself.

BIBLIOGRAPHY

The following books were either useful sources of reference or make recommended reading. With so many books available the list is not intended to be definitive, but merely a small selection of those we came across during our research.

MILLS, A.D.	*DORSET PLACE NAMES.*	ROY GASSON ASSOCIATES, 1986
HOSKINS, W.G.	*DEVON.*	DAVID & CHARLES, 1972
PAGE, J.L.W.	*THE RIVERS OF DEVON.*	SEELEY AND CO.LTD, 1893
PULMAN, G.	*THE BOOK OF THE AXE.*	KINGSMEAD REPRINTS, 1969
WILLS, G.	*DEVON ESTUARIES.*	DEVON BOOKS, 1992
D.F of W.I.	*THE DEVON VILLAGE BOOK.*	COUNTRYSIDE BOOKS, 1990
BERRY, L.	*AROUND AXMINSTER IN OLD PHOTOGRAPHS.*	SUTTON, 1993
BARNS, N	*THE EAST DEVON WAY*	EDDC, 1993.

PART 4
USEFUL INFORMATION

Tourist Information Centres

Chard	The Guildhall, Fore Street, Chard, Somerset, TA20 1PP	01460 67463
Axminster	The Old Courthouse, Church Street, Axminster, EX13 5AQ	01297 34386
Seaton	The Underfleet, Seaton, Devon, EX12 2TB	01297 21660

District Councils

East Devon DC	The Knowle, Station Road, Sidmouth, Devon, EX10 8HL	01395 516551
West Dorset DC	58-60 High West Street, Dorchester, Dorset, DT1 1UZ	01305 251010
South Somerset DC	Brympton Way, Yeovil, Somerset, BA20 2HT	01935 462462

Taxis

National Taxi Hotline		0800 654321
Axminster	BJ's Taxis	01297 35007
	Males Taxis	01297 34000
Colyton	East Devon Taxis	01297 552216
Crewkerne	Crewkerne Taxis	01460 75088
Seaton	Sovereign Cars	01297 23000
	Clapps Taxis	01297 20038 / 23366
Chard	Kings/B&W Taxis	01460 68400
	Merlin Taxis	01460 67007
Bridport	Express Cabs	01308 422288
	Pats Cabs	01308 424715
	King Cabs	01308 425489
	Abacus	01308 423455
	Acorn	01308 422422
	Bills Taxis	01308 422806
	Beeline	01308 425555
Beaminster	Beaminster Taxis	01308 862894
	Greenways	01308 862493

Public Transport (Rail Services and Operator)

South West Trains	Daily	London - **Crewkerne (Misterton)** - **Axminster**-Exeter.
South West Trains Ltd		01703 213600

Private Tram Service and Operator

Seaton Tramway	Daily (Not every day in winter)	**Seaton - Colyford** - Colyton
Seaton Tramway	Harbour Road, Seaton, Devon, EX12 2NQ	01297 20375

Public Transport (Bus Operators)

Devon Bus Enquiry Line		01392 382800
Dorset Bus Enquiry Line		01305 225165
Somerset Bus Enquiry Line		01823 255696
National Rail Enquiries		08497 484950
National Express Coach Services		08705 808080
Axe Valley Mini Travel	26 Harbour Road, Seaton, EX12 2NA	01297 625959
Stagecoach Devon	Bus Station, Paris Street, Exeter	01392 427711
First Southern National	Bus Station, Taunton, TA1 4AF	01823 272033
Cooks Coaches	White Ball Garage, Wellington, TA21 OLT	01297 32449
Mike Halford	Kisem, North Mills, Bridport, DT6 3AH	01308 421106
Sewards Coaches	Glendale, Dalwood, Axminster, EX13 7EJ	01404 881343
Stennings	Merriottsford Garage, Merriott, TA15 5NH	01460 75089

Public Transport (Bus Services)

The following services were available at the time of going to press but you should check the current status with the operator or council enquiry line as they are liable to change without much notice. Also not all services use the "route number" and some services use a different number dependent upon which County Timetable booklet they appear in.

No	Operator	Frequency	Route
20	First Southern National	Weekdays	Taunton-Honiton-**Colyton-Colyford-Seaton**
31	First Southern National	Daily	Taunton-Chard-Perry Street-**Weycroft-**Axminster-Lyme Regis-Dorchester-Weymouth
40	First Southern National	Weekdays	Bridport-**Beaminster**
47	First Southern National	Weekdays (+ Suns in Summer)	Bridport-**Beaminster-Mosterton-**Misterton-Crewkerne-Yeovil
X53	First Southern National	Weekdays	Exeter-**Seaton-Colyford-**Lyme Regis-Bridport
378	First Southern National	Sundays	Sidmouth-**Seaton-**Lyme Regis
D84	Stennings	Tue, Thur, Friday	**Beaminster-Mosterton/Clapton-**Crewkerne
621	Stennings	Friday	Crewkerne-Misterton-**Mosterton**
885	Axe Valley MT	Weekdays	**Seaton-Colyford-Colyton-Whitford-Axminster**
899	Axe Valley MT	Weekdays	Sidmouth-**Seaton-Axmouth-**Lyme Regis
380	Stagecoach Devon	Weekdays	**Axminster-Kilmington-**Honiton-Exeter
689	Stagecoach Devon	Tuesday	Honiton-**Kilmington-Axminster-Chard Junction-**Chard
688	Sewards	Thursday	**Axminster-Tytherleigh-**Perry Street-**Chard Junction-**Thorncombe-Axminster
903	Sewards	Wednesday	**Seaton-Colyford-Colyton-Whitford-Axminster-Tytherleigh-**Chard-Taunton
904	Sewards	Wednesday	**Axminster-Tytherleigh-**Perry Street-**Chard Junction-**Thorncombe-Bridport
685	Cooks Coaches	Weekdays	Taunton-Chard-**Winsham-Clapton-**Crewkerne-Ilminster
55/73	Mike Halford	Weekdays	Bridport-**Beaminster**